About the Author

Hello readers, my name is Lee and in the spiritual realms I am known as the messenger Oanedus. After my engineering apprenticeship I spent my early years studying mechanical drafting, thermal engineering and electronics and my latter years studying hypnosis and counselling; theology and finally metaphysics.

I first became aware of my psychic abilities in my early twenties though did not realize or utilize their potential for many years, until the year 1986, when early one morning I awoke from sleep to find myself levitating horizontally above the bed, with two mysterious spirit entities present.

The younger one of the two stood beside me at the side of the bed instructing and advising me about my future for nearly half an hour, while the older, sagely looking one sat on a wooden chair next to the door listening to, commenting on, and observing the proceedings.

This unusual encounter led me into a serious study of the paranormal, so that by 1990 I became proficient enough in this endeavour to summon any spirit entity or angel directly to me from the spirit world and communicate freely with them. This pursuit finally led to direct communication with God.

By relating some of my supernatural encounters and experiences, I trust that you, the reader will find this rare insight into the hidden world of angels provided herein, valuable and informative.

Thereby, I present it to you in all sincerity in the hope of helping you in your own personal spiritual growth and development by giving you a greater insight into, and a better understanding of the seven spiritual realms and the nine houses of angels outlined for you in this book.

Interviewing Guardian Angels

with
Comments from

God

&

Archangels

By

Lee Anthony Looby PhD

Malakh House

Malakh House
Mentone Victoria 3194
Copyright © Lee Looby 2004
Proof printed by Solutions Digital 2006
Published 2012

Lulu Press Inc. 2012

~ Cataloguing in Publication Entry ~

Looby, Lee -1948-
Interviewing Guardian Angels: with comments from God & archangels

Bibliography.

Includes index.

ISBN 978-0-9806232-3-9

1. Guardian angels. 2. Archangels. I. Title.

235.3

Non-Fiction

English (United States)

This book is sold subject to the condition that it not be reproduced or transmitted in its entirety by any means or in any form without the prior permission of the copyright holder or publisher, except in the case of brief quotations embodied in critical articles or reviews. All rights reserved.

Lulu Press Inc.

2012

Interviewing Guardian Angels

with

God
&
Archangels

by

the messenger
Oanedus

This skywriting pre-empts the appearance of the Son of Man.

The photograph is the first of three that were taken of the skywriting, 'Jesus ♥ u,' two of which are reproduced here for the reader.

Contrary to the color of the photo, the sky was bright blue on the day with little cloud cover.

See page xvi for the second photo in this sequence.

Table of Contents

Dedication from Yahweh
ix

Your Guardian Angel
xi

Guardian Angels Residing in the Nine Celestial Houses
xvii

The Kingdom of God
xx

The Ten Requirements
xxiii

A Foreword from Yahweh
xxv

The Beginning
1

More Angels
7

Interviewing Guardian Angels
11

The Archangel Gabriel
21

The Archangel Michael
190

The Last Pages
195

Glossary
203

Index
209

Bibliography
219

Behold! This is the eye of God for all to see.

Let it be seen that God has arrived in His heavenly glory to instruct us and to take control of the earth once more.

This photo was taken on 26th April 2002, in Gippsland, Victoria, Australia, with the permission of the property owner, a childhood friend of the author's father.

The property was originally called, 'Angel's Rest.'

Yahweh was not visible to the naked eye at the time the photograph was taken.

Dedication from Yahweh

This book is written for and dedicated to the faithful few who believe in me, the God who is here and the God of all things great and small.

I would like all who read this book to know that the one and only God who created all things including all life, is alive and watching over you.

My life is for you and I dedicate my life to you too.

I have been away but am now back as it is close to the time of Judgment and it is going to be upon you shortly.

My angels are always working tirelessly to keep you all happy and they are here to be called upon whenever you need them.

The reason for this book is to let you know that a larger book is due out soon with my words in and it will be called, *'The Word.'*

My messenger Lee will be doing this for you and for me and the proceeds shall be distributed among the poor. And the poor will then read 'The Word' and they will be saved.

Your loving Father,

Yahweh.

Interviewing Guardian Angels

Guardian angel on duty

This is the angel Luhian who is a messenger from the House of Seraphim. Passing by on his duties, he saved the four occupants of this vehicle from death and injury. All four miraculously walked away without a scratch.

Luhian was at hand immediately prior to impact as he had heard one of the panicked occupants cry out in fright.

Photo courtesy of Shawna Platt, a widely known and well respected psychic. The photo was posted on her former Website, 'The Guardian Angel Community,' by a member of her group.

The photograph is said to have originated from the Washington State Police Department, USA.

Your Guardian Angel

House of Seraphim   Page 11

Looks after those born: -

Vehuiah	-21 March to 25 March	page 11
Jeliel	-26 March to 30 March	page 12
Sitael	-31 March to 04 April	page 13
Elemiah	-05 April to 09 April	page 14
Mahasiah	-10 April to 14 April	page 15
Lelahel	-15 April to 20 April	page 16
Achaiah	-21 April to 25 April	page 18
Cahetel	-26 April to 30 April	page 19

House of Cherubim   Page 22

Looks after those born: -

Haziel	-01 May to 05 May	page 22
Aladiah	-06 May to 10 May	page 23
Lauviah	-11 May to 15 May	page 24
Hahaiah	-16 May to 20 May	page 26
Iezalel	-21 May to 25 May	page 28
Mebahel	-26 May to 31 May	page 30
Hariel	-01 June to 05 June	page 31
Hekamiah	-06 June to 10 June	page 35

Your Guardian Angel

House of Thrones   **Page 38**

Looks after those born: -

Lahuiah	-11 June to 15 June	page 38
Caliel	-16 June to 21 June	page 40
Leuviah	-22 June to 26 June	page 43
Pahaliah	-27 June to 01 July	page 44
Nelchael	-02 July to 06 July	page 46
Yeiayel	-07 July to 11 July	page 47
Melahel	-12 July to 16 July	page 50
Hahuiah	-17 July to 22 July	page 51

House of Dominions   **Page 54**

Looks after those born: -

Nithaiah	-23 July to 27 July	page 54
Ahaiah	-28 July to 01 August	page 57
Yeratel	-02 August to 06 August	page 59
Sehaiah	-07 August to 12 August	page 60
Reiyel	-13 August to 17 August	page 62
Omael	-18 August to 22 August	page 65
Lecabel	-23 August to 28 August	page 67
Vasaiah	-29 August to 02 September	page 68

Your Guardian Angel

House of Virtues   Page 71

Looks after those born: -

Yehuiah	-03 September to 07 September	page 71
Lehahiah	-08 September to 12 September	page 73
Chavakiah	-13 September to 17 September	page 75
Menadel	-18 September to 23 September	page 77
Haniel	-24 September to 28 September	page 79
Haamiah	-29 September to 03 October	page 82
Rehael	-04 October to 08 October	page 83
Ieiazel	-09 October to 13 October	page 85

House of Powers   Page 88

Looks after those born: -

Hahahel	-14 October to 18 October	page 88
Mikael	-19 October to 23 October	page 91
Veuliah	-24 October to 28 October	page 98
Yelahiah	-29 October to 02 November	page 100
Sehaliah	-03 November to 07 November	page 103
Ariel	-08 November to 12 November	page 109
Asaliah	-13 November to 17 November	page 112
Mihael	-18 November to 22 November	page 115

Interviewing Guardian Angels

Your Guardian Angel

House of Principalities   Page 121

Looks after those born: -

Vehuel	-23 November to 27 November	page 121
Daniel	-28 November to 02 December	page 124
Hahasiah	-03 December to 07 December	page 126
Imamiah	-08 December to 12 December	page 128
Nanael	-13 December to 16 December	page 130
Nithael	-17 December to 21 December	page 132
Mebahiah	-22 December to 26 December	page 134
Poyel	-27 December to 31 December	page 137

House of Archangels   Page 140

Looks after those born: -

Nemamiah	-01 January to 05 January	page 140
Yeialel	-06 January to 10 January	page 141
Harael	-11 January to 15 January	page 147
Mitzrael	-16 January to 20 January	page 149
Umabel	-21 January to 25 January	page 152
Iahhel	-26 January to 30 January	page 154
Anael	-31 January to 04 February	page 157
Mehiel	-05 February to 09 February	page 160

Interviewing Guardian Angels

Your Guardian Angel

House of Angels **Page 164**

Looks after those born: -

Damabiah	-10 February to 15 February	page 164
Manakel	-16 February to 20 February	page 166
Eyael	-21 February to 25 February	page 169
Habuiah	-26 February to 28 February and 29 February each leap year.	page 171
Rochel	-01 March to 05 March	page 175
Jabamiah	-06 March to 10 March	page 179
Haiahel	-11 March to 15 March	page 181
Mumiah	-16 March to 20 March	page 185

This photo of a love heart was taken from the backyard of the author in broad daylight, a bright sunny day in August, 2002.

It is the second photograph in a set of three taken on the same day, of skywriting formed by an airplane which took off from Moorabbin Airport in Victoria, Australia.

The sky, though bright blue came out completely different in each one. The sun at the time was 90 degrees to the right. The radiant presence of Jesus enveloping the heart was not visible to the naked eye at the time

Guardian Angels Residing in the Nine Celestial Houses

The House of Seraphim

Vehuiah Jeliel Sitael

Elemiah Mahasiah Lelahel

Achaiah Cahetel

The House of Cherubim

Haziel Aladiah Lauviah

Hahaiah Iezalel Mebahel

Hariel Hekamiah

The House of Thrones

Lahuiah Caliel Leuviah

Pahaliah Nelchael Yeiayel

Melahel Hahuiah

Guardian Angels Residing in the Nine Celestial Houses

The House of Dominions

Nithaiah Ahaiah Yeratel

Sehaiah Reiyel Omael

Lecabel Vasaiah

The House of Virtues

Yehuiah Lehahiah Chavakiah

Menadel Haniel Haamiah

Rehael Ieiazel

The House of Powers

Hahahel Mikael Veuliah

Yelahiah Sehaliah Ariel

Asaliah Mihael

Guardian Angels Residing in the Nine Celestial Houses

The House of Principalities

Vehuel   Daniel   Hahasiah

Imamiah   Nanael   Nithael

Mebahiah   Poyel

The House of Archangels

Nemamiah   Yeialel   Harael

Mitzrael   Umabel   Iahhel

Anael   Mehiel

The House of Angels

Damabiah   Manakel   Eyael

Habuiah   Rochel   Jabamiah

Haiahel   Mumiah

Interviewing Guardian Angels

Kingdom of God

Outline of Non-Physical Realms

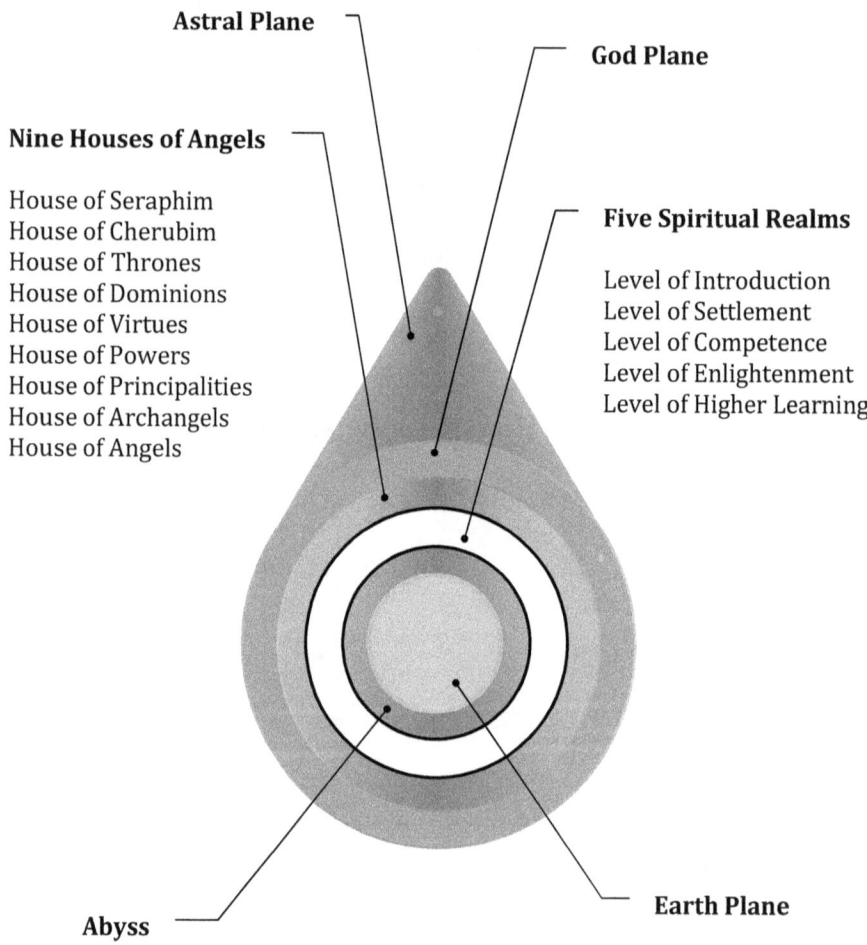

Astral Plane

God Plane

Nine Houses of Angels

House of Seraphim
House of Cherubim
House of Thrones
House of Dominions
House of Virtues
House of Powers
House of Principalities
House of Archangels
House of Angels

Five Spiritual Realms

Level of Introduction
Level of Settlement
Level of Competence
Level of Enlightenment
Level of Higher Learning

Earth Plane

Abyss

The Five Spiritual Realms are known as 'The Light.'
The Earth Plane depicted is a non-physical realm and is not part of the light though is regarded as one of the seven heavenly realms.

God says, "Let me say a few words to you, reading this. I will tell you that it is important for you to have your life ready to be examined in detail, and you will be examined in detail too.

"Let me remind you, this is my way of telling you without you having to go to anyone else or to anywhere else to find out about me. And this is why I am telling you here, as I have no other option than to have you read it here.

"Let me state emphatically that I will be looking at you to see if you are ready to come home to me, and to see if you are worthy of entering the place that I have prepared for you.

"Let me add, that if you obey my rules and keep the peace, then I will embrace you, otherwise your future is not guaranteed to be the one you have in mind, but rather, the one I have in mind.

"My angels are here because they have been proven worthy.

"And if you are proven worthy then your future is going to be one of the best imaginable, so strive to be here in my house living in the lap of my luxury; and the gifts that I have prepared so well and so lovingly for you will be yours to keep."

Father

This photo of the author enveloped by a rainbow was taken on 27th April, 2002, at the site of the now defunct Riverview Tea Gardens, Avondale Heights, Victoria, Australia.

It was a fine sunny afternoon without any hint of rain. The rainbow, which is a symbolic bridge between the physical and spiritual realms, was not visible to the naked eye. The east-west rectangular plinth being knelt upon is all that remains of a statue, a replica Venus de Milo which once faced east toward the Maribyrnong River.

The Venus de Milo was ruined when a fire swept through the gardens in early 1968 and has only recently been replaced with another statue, facing north, called 'The White Lady.'

Built on 5 acres of a 112 acre allotment, the tea gardens were originally established diagonally adjacent to the river in 1909, on old Wurundjeri tribal grounds, by entrepreneur Daniel Hicks.

The Ten Requirements

Spiritual enlightenment comes from a combination of thought, word and deed.

The enlightened one must possess and utilize the following attributes.

The ability to forgive.

The ability to help those in need.

The ability to love.

The ability to show kindness to those in need, whether man or beast.

The ability to ask God for forgiveness.

The ability to generously help the poor.

The ability to give of yourself when others require help.

The ability to find time to care for the sick and the elderly.

The ability to ask for help so that you also may live.

The ability to seek guidance in spiritual matters and be true to yourself.

Archangel Omni

~

Yahweh is back!

Yahweh has been absent but is now back, watching over us.

This photograph was taken by the author on 26 April, 2002, and is of a building once used as a private museum in Gippsland, Victoria, Australia.

The owners were showing us around their property, though were unaware of Yahweh's presence at the time.

Yahweh had promised me earlier, in 2001, that He would appear in the next set of outdoor photographs that I took.

A Foreword from Yahweh

1. Let me begin by stating that I am the God of Abraham, Isaac, Jacob and Jesus too.
2. Let me tell you truthfully, my plans include you and I will let you know what they are soon.
3. Let all understand that my Son will be here too. And he will run the world as he is to be in charge once he arrives.
4. Let it be seen that my Son will take control of the world and he will distribute the wealth. And he will see that all are fed and clothed and have a roof over their heads.
5. My plans will eventuate gradually and he will look after you. So do not concern yourself with this as it has been planned for centuries.
6. And it will run to my plans, not to the plans of humankind and not to the plans of world leaders either as they will be in front of me, explaining themselves.
7. I will let you know what my decisions are regarding them and you will all see justice done.
8. My long term plan is to get you into the realms that you are destined for according to your level of spiritual awareness, and for you to be put into the same category as all of those at the same thinking level.

9. And this will make it a pleasant place to be as not one will be cleverer than the other.
10. Let it happen that you are to be put into the best place for your aptitude, and this is my plan as your life will be put to the test.
11. And you will have many ways of determining what my best plan is for you and what you will want to do for me.
12. And I will accomplish this in the time allowed, and the time allowed is to be one thousand years.
13. Let it be seen then that you are to be placed into a house with many others.
14. And your bed will be one of silk and roses; your quilt will be of the finest linen, your mattress will be of the finest down and your life will be one of the best imaginable.
15. And the life that you will have decided that you should have is up to you.
16. And you will have many choices as this is my way, and I have decided to give you any amount of choices.
17. And if you find one is too difficult, go to a level that is suitable for you.
18. Then go to the Level of Competence to find out what the scholars have in mind and watch them do their work, and they will be watching you too.
19. Let it be known that you are one of my children and let it be seen that I have been watching you, and I will be watching you in the future too.

20. Let me tell you now that I know all about you. And it is not important what you have done but what you have not done, as it will be looked at.
21. And all the work left undone will be done and all the chores left undone will be done, and all the words left unspoken will be spoken too.
22. Let me tell you that I have been here since the beginning, and it has been a long time in my eyes too. And if you think in terms of years, tell me what it would seem like to you, to live forever.
23. Let it be known that my plans include this longevity for you. And let me tell you that this longevity is everlasting; not the life you have now, but a life of creation.
24. And your life of all-lasting will never end as you are to live until it is not known what time is, and what life was.
25. And this will never be, so your life will not ever be extinguished, and your flame will linger on forever.
26. Let it be that my plans will come to fruition by coming home to me and asking me to let you into my house.
27. And if you find this too difficult then I can only say that your fate rests on your own shoulders, as your life is in your own hands, not mine.
28. And it will soon become obvious that this is to be sooner rather that later, so please do this for me as well as for yourself.

29. Let me tell you that one day you will be here in my place doing this for those you have created; and you will develop into what I am as you are made in my image.

30. And if you want this, come home to me with your arms outstretched; and if you do not want this, turn away and do not finish reading as you are wasting my time and have decided already that you are not worthy.

31. So those of you who are still reading are those who want this. And those of you who want this are my beloved children, and this is the reward that I have made ready for you.

32. This is my final word on it today so let it be seen that my words are the words of the living God, Yahweh.

33. And I am the God of all there is, all that ever was, and all there ever will be!

Your loving Father,

Yahweh.

The Beginning

Early one morning in 1986 I experienced an extraordinary event, in that two heavenly messengers appeared to me during a supernatural levitation which awoke me from my slumbers.

One of the angels spoke to me, albeit tersely, strongly advising me to resign from the Air Force as soon as my six year term of engagement expired as I had important work to do. At length, the angel informed me that my path was eventually to become a spiritual messenger.

After this epochal encounter I started a few years of private study into the paranormal as well as metaphysics and have now been channeling daily since 1990, regularly conversing with demons; earth bound spirits, lost souls; spirits, spirit guides; angels, guardian angels; archangels and more recently, since the year 2000, with God.

At first this channeling was just communicating with ordinary deceased souls left on the earth plane who were unable to access the light, due to their misdeeds whilst living on earth as human beings. These earth bound souls are what are commonly referred to as evil spirits, or are sometimes mistakenly called demons. (Only fallen angels who exert influence over people are actually demons).

After these first few contacts, I soon realized that most of the earth bound souls are deceptive tricksters and pathological liars, the same as they would have been when alive on earth. Now any information they offer me is taken with a grain of salt and communicating with them is more or less for counseling them only, usually about their situation in death or else bringing their living relatives into contact with them.

Notwithstanding, I still sought to have contact with higher spirits and spirit guides living in the light which I did eventually. After that the information and opinions I received on different topics became much

The Beginning

better and far more reliable than any I had previously channeled from any soul left on the earth plane. It wasn't long though before I found that even in the light, in general, the spirits' range of knowledge was only about the equivalent of the average person's and they were simply expressing personal opinion rather than giving me anything unknown or profound. I quickly realized that to find more reliable and knowledgeable answers to the type of information I sought, I would have to ask at an even higher level, surpassing the light.

To communicate at all levels in the hierarchy of angels and with God was not very easy at first, as I found that to communicate freely with them I had to attain a much higher level of spiritual awareness, which I did eventually, by passing a series of fifteen tests.

My principal spirit guide Ollse arranged these tests for me over a period of forty days and forty nights and I passed all of them, attaining the highest possible level of spiritual awareness available, that being level seven in the spirit world, known as the God plane, which then enabled me to communicate directly with God. These tests were designed specifically to see how ethically and morally I would react and respond in certain situations and to certain questions and events.

I was rather curious to find out what all these levels in the light were called, so asked Ollse to name them for me. He told me that level one on the earth plane, though a spiritual realm, is not actually a level in the light at all. This is how he explained it to me.

"Lee, level one in the spiritual realms is on the earth plane and souls who have not attained any enlightenment are left to dwell on this plane, the same plane people live on. Souls left on the earth plane in spirit cannot see, nor can they hear, but can communicate with others mainly by thought transfer known as telepathy. Another common

The Beginning

means of communication they have with humans is through spirit mediums also known as channelers and three widely used methods spirits have of communicating with people are through clairvoyance, trance channeling and automatic-writing, though many other means are also employed. However, these three seem to be the most common."

Some spirit mediums prefer or need to go into a trance and then let the spirits speak out through their mouth, though personally I always remain fully alert when communicating, much preferring to use telepathy or, if I want to keep a record of the conversation, auto-write it down with a pen or auto-type it down on the computer.

It is very easy for most people to communicate with lowly earth bound spirits or with demons, though I would not recommend deliberately contacting them as telling lies is their forte, leading people astray with misinformation, bringing problems into their lives.

Unfortunately, lowly spirits are the easiest to contact as they make up about 70% of deceased souls on the other side. That is the reason why the prophet Moses warned his people, the Hebrew people; not to delve into spiritism, now commonly referred to as 'spiritualism;' for their own sake and if you have a Bible handy, look it up and read his words.[1]

The first and foremost important law of communicating with spirits is to always ask the entity you are contacting if they are from the light. Earth bound spirits are compelled to give you the correct answer if you ask where they reside, for reasons that I will divulge later.

People cannot contact spirits who are at a higher level of spiritual awareness than they are at; that is, operating at a higher level of

---

[1] See (Deuteronomy 18:10 -12)

The Beginning

spirituality than they have attained, most only being able to contact those souls who remain bound on the earth plane. With the many different levels in the light, when a person dies, their soul is transported to the level they have attained, by the purity of the thoughts, words and deeds they have displayed throughout their lifetime.

Here is a list of seven relevant levels as presented to me by Ollse.

Level One	**The Earth Plane**
Level Two	**The Level of Introduction**
Level Three	**The Level of Settlement**
Level Four	**The Level of Competence**
Level Five	**The Level of Enlightenment**
Level Six	**The Level of Higher Learning**
Level Seven	**The God Plane**

The final level, level seven is the God plane in the Kingdom of God, and this is probably why the term 'seventh heaven' is used to describe a state of euphoria by some.

The astral plane is different again. It is the pathway where souls travel during meditation or sleep, enabling them to reach the angelic realms or the light. However, the majority of people who enter the astral plane are not evolved enough spiritually to enter the houses of angels or non-physical spiritual realms in the light and these people simply astral travel on the earth plane or travel to other parts of the universe.

The astral plane, not being part of the light but rather the access channel to the light (through a portal within the nucleus of the mind), is a universal dimension where people travel in their dreams and travel during meditation from one realm to another. It is the place where thoughts travel when communicating with others clairvoyantly or by

The Beginning

telepathy and a place where positive and negative thought forms gather, to be dissipated by God's angels by cancelling these positive and negative energies out. Negative energy thought-forms from the astral plane can manifest and attack the living, as in psychic attack, so must be dissipated regularly.

I have found that souls residing in the lower levels of the light, with the exception of souls left on level one; the earth plane,[2] (which is not part of the light); are able to attain higher levels by volunteering to become spirit guides to people still living on earth, and are eventually promoted to higher levels in the light by doing this work.

Most people have at least three spirit guides helping them in their daily tasks, with the most advanced guide assuming the role of principal guide. Angels however, not having been born as human beings reside in separate houses yet again. God has told me that no ordinary human soul resides with Him on level seven yet, as this plane is reserved for those entering His personal house on their Judgment Day. Therefore, going to the light in the kingdom of heaven is not the same as entering the God plane in the Kingdom of God, i.e., level seven.[3]

Not long after passing these tests I started speaking to a couple of archangels (who are messengers between God, angels and people on earth) and Archangel Gabriel asked me if I would like to tell people about their guardian angels and spirit guides.

Gabriel wanted me to inform the people that, "... each person has their very own guardian angel assigned to them at the time of birth, as

---

[2] Only lost souls residing on the earth plane are allowed to enter the light when they are ready. All others left on the earth plane will remain there until Judgment Day.

[3] God refers to His personal house on the 'God plane' as His 'kingdom,' in the kingdom of God. The Kingdom of God includes 'all of that is' but for this exercise will specifically mean God's personal dwelling place, on the God plane.

The Beginning

this is the time the soul enters the prepared physical living body, bringing spiritual awareness to it."

The very first angel that I ever asked to speak to as a messenger was Archangel Gabriel, and frankly I had only heard of the names of Gabriel and Michael then, as my knowledge of angels and archangels was almost non-existent, especially when it came to knowing anything about what they did or anything about their busy working lives.

Since then, I have discovered and spoken to a few more archangels. These archangels reside in one of the nine celestial houses alongside the other guardian angels from that house and are in charge of all the houses and spiritual realms in heaven.

As well as carrying out many other important duties, some archangels are rostered on duty as messengers during the week, though this routine is variable and changes regularly.

Over a period of time, especially during the last few years, I have had the privilege of speaking to many more of the angels and have befriended them. The dialog in the following pages is from seventy-two of the guardian angels that I have spoken to and I have asked them all to provide me with a little insight into their daily lives.

Now that I can also communicate directly with God whose name is Yahweh, He has asked me to write some of His words down to include here in this book.

Yahweh has written a brief introduction to each of His nine houses of angels and has given a general description of their main duties, outlining their heavenly roles as well as making other invaluable contributions throughout the book.

More Angels

The nine houses of angels are directly beneath the God plane and directly adjacent to the five spiritual realms known as the light, these only being separated from each other by gates. Some angels refer to all of their houses as being part of the light, regarding themselves as being from the light. There are three separate angelic levels each containing three houses, and until recently, only seventy-two guardian angels resided in the nine celestial houses along with the other angels and archangels that make up this hierarchy.

There are numerous other angel types as well as the guardians residing in the nine houses and all are assigned specific duties to carry out. In fact there are so many angels that the total number is impossible to say with any accuracy, but I would estimate somewhere between seven and eight million, each one having an individual role to play.

Not many really when you consider that the earth's population is well and truly over six billion living souls, heading toward seven with approximately ten billion deceased souls in all of the various spiritual realms, many vying for reincarnation.

After speaking to dozens of guardian angels over a period of several weeks, it soon became apparent to me that they were all working far too hard and needed help to carry out their many and varied duties. Therefore, on their behalf, I asked Yahweh to provide three angel helpers for each one of them to help out wherever and whenever necessary, as those I had already spoken to told me they were on a tight schedule and couldn't stay to speak to me for very long due to their heavy workload. Shortly after this, I saw that they still needed much more help than just a few temporary, intermittent helpers, so asked

Yahweh if He would provide the three helpers to each of them on a permanent basis. Yahweh approved this request on 7th December 2000.

On speaking to these angels again and subsequently to other angels later on, I asked if the extra help was sufficient to cover demand for their services and most replied that they were still unable to cope with the workload in front of them, even with all of the help they were now getting, due to the rapid changes happening in the world.

Seeing they were still overloaded with work and receiving many requests for help, I once again asked Yahweh to allocate each of the seventy-two guardian angels with yet another three helpers.

That day, on 25th December 2000, each guardian angel received another three helpers, bringing the total number of permanent helpers each had to six. Even so, not long after this, I realized that these six helpers were still not going to be enough to carry out all of the requests for help people were asking of them, as well as performing all of their other celestial duties. So, on the strength of this observation, I asked Yahweh to supply a further six helpers for each of them.

On 7th June 2001, each angel was allotted six more helpers on a permanent basis, bringing the total number each now had to twelve. The number of guardian angels had increased, therefore, from the original seventy-two, to nine hundred and thirty six in just on six months.

A further development happened on 7th July, 2001. Even with this many guardian angels, there were still not enough to answer all the calls for help and to attend to all the emergencies happening worldwide. After further discussions with Yahweh, He decided to allow the angels an unlimited number of helpers from thereon in to cope with the upcoming events that are foreseen in the future, mainly pending wars and natural disasters.

Utilizing this incredible ability I now have to communicate directly with the angels and with God, I started to ask for and receive information that I felt would be of interest to some acquaintances of mine. I was then able to give these people the names of their own guardian angels, and to give them a brief outline of the duties these angels performed, as well as providing them with some other interesting information about their own angel's role and personal life.

Therefore I have attempted to bring to you, the reader; a running knowledge of what is known to me about the guardian angels residing in the nine celestial houses, in their own environment; trying to explain how they operate by providing a little window into their personal lives.

Each introduction given to me here is directly channeled from the angel whose name appears herein, with a brief statement outlining the duties they carry out; and wherever possible, a little information about their activities and hobbies; letting you, the reader see into their different personalities, giving you an insight into the wide and diverse range of the weird and wonderful duties they carry out.

As a matter of interest, angels and spirits residing in the spiritual realms do not sleep and can communicate instantly with anyone anywhere. That is the reason why, when they are communicating with anyone they always include the person's first name, so that there is no mistake as to whom they are addressing; as all other spirits can listen into the conversation if they want to, unless there is a specific need to keep it private.

The spirit medium can stop other spirits from eavesdropping and can have a confidential conversation by asking to be surrounded by God's protective white light; then no other entity can enter that medium's private space and listen into or join in on the conversation.

More Angels

Now, here is an account of the guardian angels that are here looking after us in our daily lives. By no means are these the names of all the guardian angels now residing in the spiritual realms, just the names of the original seventy-two we first started off with.

God says, "My plans will be seen soon though they are not the sort of plans you would expect. My world is not your world though your world is my world, but not in the same way you think.

"The world will be changed forever and this will be the beginning for all remaining alive on earth and in heaven. Let me explain that this is really the beginning for you if you are willing to be my loved and cherished child, and you want to be here to have my comforting love and my house to live in.

"Let it be seen then that I have given you every chance to make it into my house; and if you think you cannot find me, try to have the last say in it and speak to me directly, and you will be heard.

"My love is unending as the universe is unending and I will give you plenty to think about and do in this new time and new place you will be in. So keep my words in mind and think about them for your own sake, not mine; and be sure to have my book in your house to read too.

"My book was written centuries ago to let you know about me and my Son; and you will be able to find us in the future, not the past. Look to this time in the future when we will be together and you will have plenty to look forward to, in my house with me."

Interviewing Guardian Angels

Guardian angels look after those born within a specific time frame.

House of Seraphim

Guardian angels residing in this house look after those born
- 21st March to 30th April -

God says, "Angels residing in this house are my sentries, and they are the ones who guard all the gates and keep order in the houses. They also keep their eye on the spirits who need to be transferred from one realm to the next."

VEHUIAH - looks after those born on 21st March to 25th March.

"Lee, it is Vehuiah."
"Hello Vehuiah, are you an angel from the House of Seraphim?"
"Yes, I am the angel who looks after the house when all are out, to make sure none enter here who should not be here, and I also keep the house records for later on. When called upon I give assistance to those in need and give healing when required, as well as giving of my time to appease those found in dire circumstances by showing them the options available to them. I also give my love to those who feel the need to be uplifted and give the required help to those seeking assistance when they pray to Father, who sends me to help."
"Have you any more to add to that, Vehuiah?"
"I would like to add that I also give my time to the spirit guides bringing fresh souls to the spiritual realms, and that I give assistance to those

Chapter 1. House of Seraphim

souls having a difficult time adjusting to the spirit world, as some are really traumatized; not by their own deaths, but by the hurt they see in the faces of those left behind."

"I also like to go to the beach and watch the boats in the harbor as they are my favorite pastime, and I love to see them sailing; and it is a pleasure to see the people enjoying the beaches and having picnics."

"Thanks Vehuiah, goodbye."

"Goodbye Lee and thanks for the time and effort you are putting into this for us."

JELIEL - looks after those born on 26th March to 30th March.

"Lee it is me, Jeliel."

"Are you the angel Jeliel from the House of Seraphim?"

"Yes Lee, I am your angel friend to whom you have spoken to many times before, about the people. I am here to give you any information about me and my duties you need to know, to write about in your book about all of us, to tell to those who seek the truth.

"I am the angel who takes measures to ensure that people are able to contact their loved ones after they have died. I give them messages of love and pass on information to them much the same as messengers and archangels do at a higher level, except the people I contact are usually of a psychic nature and can easily hear me."

"Thanks, Jeliel, how do you pass the information on to them?"

"It is by impressing the messages into their minds during sleep, as they are relaxed and can receive messages better then than when they are awake and alert. My duties are mainly in the work of our Father and I would not consider doing any other type of work as I love doing this, and

Chapter 1. House of Seraphim

it gives me the job satisfaction that comes only when you are very happy."

"Jeliel, what do you do in your spare time?"

"I go to the hospitals and see if it is time to take any home, and they are usually ready as their spirit guides are there to help them in this too; and we take particularly good care of them to ease the transition from one plane to the next."

"Thanks Jeliel, I will speak to you again shortly, goodbye for now."

"Thank you too Lee and I look forward to hearing from you again, goodbye."

SITAEL - looks after those born on 31st March to 4th April.

"Lee it is Sitael!"

"Hello Sitael, are you an angel from the House of Seraphim?"

"Yes, I am an angel of the Lord God and I am the main one here in the House of Seraphim. I am the angel who disciplines those who take the wrong path and I am the angel who punishes those who do not come up to my expectations. And I am the angel who administers this punishment. And I give it out with the daily bread as those who eat of it and drink from my font are apt to realize; and I will not take any nonsense from any. And I am the one who has the power to set any soul back a peg or two if they misbehave themselves as I am a hard taskmaster, and I want all to know it!"

"What else do you do, Sitael?"

"The other duties I have entail looking after the unclean souls who are left on the earth plane awaiting their fate, and I give them plenty to think about too!"

"Thank you for your forthright duty statement Sitael!"

Chapter 1. House of Seraphim

"Lee, thank you too, for hearing me with all my workload still in front of me to bear!"

"Sitael, what about the unlimited amount of helpers assigned to help you recently?"

"Lee, they are not to my high standard and I need helpers who have strength of character and plenty of grit to do the job properly!"

"Okay, goodbye for now my friend."

"Lee, thank you for giving me the opportunity to say my piece here and God bless you."

ELEMIAH - looks after those born on 5th April to 9th April.

"Lee it is Elemiah!"

"Are you Elemiah, an angel from the House of Seraphim?"

"Yes Lee, I am the angel Elemiah and my duties are to keep the spirits fully entertained and occupied as they tend to mill about talking to each other causing disruptions to an otherwise blissful existence here. And I keep them entertained by giving them little tasks to carry out in the house, making them feel as though they are contributing by doing something worthwhile.

"This keeps them happily occupied and also gives them space to think about their future role here as they are all waiting to be judged, and all are trying to gain a higher level of spiritual awareness before the final days are upon them. And they need to get as much enlightenment as is possible, to be able to become higher beings later on."

"Okay, thanks Elemiah, is there anything else you would like to add to that?"

"Lee, I am also the one who preaches sermons to them and I play the harp as well as play other instruments to entertain them whenever they

Chapter 1. House of Seraphim

wish to have choir practice, or they simply sing songs to enjoy themselves"

"That sounds very accommodating of you, Elemiah! Thank you for this insight into your duties and I'll look forward to hearing from you again; goodbye."

"Lee, I am delighted to finally get the opportunity to thank you for arranging with our Father to have so many new helpers, as we need them now more than at any other time in the history of the human race, goodbye."

MAHASIAH -   looks after those born on 10th April to 14th April.

"Lee, it is Mahasiah!"

"Are you Mahasiah, an angel from the House of Seraphim?"

"Yes Lee, I am Mahasiah who resides in the House of Seraphim with my brethren. I love being here now, as my duties are much lighter than they were before you asked our Father to give us all the help we so sorely needed to get us through our daily tasks, which are many, believe you me!"

"What exactly are your duties, Mahasiah?"

"Lee my duties are varied, but I like to give the people I look after my undivided attention whenever I am sent to their aid as I love people, and my main concern is that they do not believe in us.

"This disappoints me when I realize they disregard us to pursue unrefined types of physical, rather than spiritual pursuits, which leaves me feeling that my work may not be regarded as worthwhile by some. But the ones who do want my help are the ones who receive the most comfort as they feel my presence. And I am able to comfort them as well

Chapter 1. House of Seraphim

as intervene in any problems facing them and also steer them toward the light, so they are able to gain enlightenment from my guidance."

"Thank you for coming here today, supplying me with this information Mahasiah."

"Lee, it is my pleasure to be here as you are a friend to all of us and we all know you. And we would all like to say our piece to you and are lucky to have you to take this information from us, as not many can. And even less can speak to our Father as far as that goes.

"Only you and the earthly messenger known as Golaiah have this privilege at the moment as the prophets are all here with us and the seers are all here too. So you are unique at the moment in that you have direct communication with our Father, as did the biblical prophets."

"Thank you Mahasiah; I'll bid you farewell for now and I hope to speak to you again shortly, goodbye."

"Lee, it is my pleasure to be able to converse with you, and we are all happy to know that you are here for us and we all appreciate your efforts; goodbye."

LELAHEL -   looks after those born on 15th April to 20th April.

"Lee, it is Lelahel!"

"Are you Lelahel, an angel from the House of Seraphim?"

"Yes Lee, I am an angel of the Lord God Almighty and I have been waiting to hear from you as all are anticipating you and wanting to speak to you about their story. All here are excited that you are writing about us and our work and we are hopeful that a few people will listen and read the words that we give you to write. We appreciate your efforts in interviewing all of us for the sake of letting the people know we are here for them, as all seem to have forgotten us and we do appreciate this as

Chapter 1. House of Seraphim

you are now aware. So we had better talk about the reason you summoned me before you and that is, to inform you what I do during my time here on earth with the other angels from the House of Seraphim."

"Yes Lelahel, that's the main reason I've asked you to speak to me today and I'd like you to give me an insight into the duties you perform, and anything else about yourself that you think may be of interest to our readers."

"Lee, I want to say that my duties are related to giving the people all the help they need to find our Father; and let those who seek Him find Him with all their heart, all their soul, and all their mind.

"And those who do not find Him have reasons of their own, but generally most have thought about God at some time or another. The ones who believe that He is here for them will reap the rewards He is providing, and those who do not believe in Him will also reap rewards of a different nature He is providing for them.

"Let me remind you that the people are looking for answers and they are willing to listen to reason. And they will find that God has called their name, and if they respond they are rewarded, and if not, they are forsaken. Let me remind those reading this, that to find God is not hard as He has found you; so why deny yourself any longer and ask Him to accept you into His heart and into His house, and your life will take on new meaning."

"Do you wish to add anything further, Lelahel?"

"Lee yes, how much do you want me to say as I can talk all day and night if you like. I have ample helpers now and they are eager to do this work so my burdens are few. I want to express my gratitude to you for asking Father to provide this extra help for us, as we were all overloaded with chores. And we had no-one to speak to our Father on our behalf until you saw, and spoke for us."

Chapter 1. House of Seraphim

"Lelahel, I'm happy that I was able to be of assistance and later on I'll ask Yahweh why He needed someone like me to ask Him to provide help to you all instead of supplying help when the need seemed obvious. Thank you for your time and I hope to speak to you again shortly, goodbye for now."

"Lee, thank you for letting us speak to the people through you, and we are going to be watching all who read our words to gauge their reactions; goodbye."

ACHAIAH -   looks after those born on 21st April to 25th April.

"Lee it is Achaiah!"

"Are you Achaiah, an angel from the House of Seraphim?"

"Yes Lee, I am the administrative angel in the house. I administer to the others, instructing them what to do during times of fire, flood, and famine and telling them who to help and who not to help. And I give the orders directly to my brethren from our Father who gives me His list to read out from the scroll of His own hand, and the scrolls which He provides us with, to instruct us with."

"Achaiah, how often does Yahweh give you the scrolls to read out to the others, with instructions showing the duties that He wants you to carry out?"

"Lee, Father gives out His scrolls every day and whenever there is an emergency He gives us specific roles, as He wants us to be as efficient as possible when we are carrying out His instructions, doing his deeds."

"What else would you like to tell me about, Achaiah?"

"Lee, I do many things as well as read out the scrolls, and we all share the responsibilities to a certain extent, as we like to help each other as well as the people we are here for. And I do a lot of visiting to keep tabs

Chapter 1. House of Seraphim

on those who are dispirited, feeling downhearted; and I bring the spirit of joy with me to make them rally, and I do this to many every day.

"Also the sick need to be made to feel happier when no-one is there to visit them, so I do and they seem to sense me there as some look quite happy once I arrive to sit next to them."

"Okay, thanks for the information Achaiah, and I trust we'll chat again shortly."

"Yes Lee, we will. As soon as you have a free moment I would like to speak to you again; goodbye."

"Okay, goodbye Achaiah."

CAHETEL -   looks after those born on 26th April to 30th April.

"I would like to speak to Cahetel; are you there, Cahetel?"

"Yes Lee, it is Cahetel!"

"Are you Cahetel, an angel from the House of Seraphim?"

"It is Cahetel, the angel from the House of Seraphim!"

"Cahetel, can you tell me about the duties you carry out and also impart a little information about yourself?"

"I am not really happy about this interview Lee, but seeing it is for the people to gain an understanding of us and how we live and what we do, I suppose it will be alright; but I do not think it is wise as the people are mainly ignorant about us and the duties we carry out, so you are probably wasting your time."

"Cahetel, I know a lot of people won't read this or even be interested, but for the ones who are interested it will prove worthwhile as they may discover a few truths that have not been available to them, or been explained to them properly, before."

Chapter 1. House of Seraphim

"Lee, the duties I carry out are to escort the souls of the dead from one realm to another whenever they are promoted from a lower level to a higher level. And they are schooled in their new environment as it is difficult at first for some to leave behind those they knew, for centuries at times and the home they had become accustomed to."

"Why are these spirits uprooted and moved to a higher spiritual realm, Cahetel?"

"It is because they have either achieved a higher level of spiritual awareness by being guides for those on earth and for those entering into the light; or, for some others, the people who love them have prayed for them and Father has forgiven them of their sins and has promoted them."

"So you mean to say that all souls in the light who have sinned on earth and have loved-ones or others pray for them to be forgiven are promoted to a higher level?"

"Usually they are Lee, if not straight away then sometime in the future when they have been here on the level for the specified time Father deems necessary."

"Can you tell me a little about yourself now, Cahetel?"

"Yes, I would like to tell you about the activities that I carry out after my main duties are over and I have time to do other things. I usually go to the House of Cherubim and update the records of those I have moved from one level to another. The Cherubim are the official record keepers but I do the records of those I have moved as I know the details, and it gives me a break away too."

"Cahetel, is there free movement between the houses of the angels?"

"Yes, for the angels there is, as we, the Seraphim are the highest house and we visit all the lower houses; however movement from lower houses to higher houses has to be approved by the sentry or gatekeeper

Chapter 1. House of Seraphim

and the reason for the visit stated. The angels are all known to each other so this is merely a formality and a chance to exchange pleasantries. The spirits can move freely within the spiritual realms below them though require permission to visit the higher realms, albeit briefly; though they only enter the houses of angels under escort to check their records at the time of death."

"Okay, thank you Cahetel; goodbye."

"Goodbye, Lee and thank you!"

"Lee, it is Gabriel from the House of Archangels!"

"Hello Gabriel! Would you like to say a few words?"

"Let me say that I am overjoyed with this work and it is a beautiful way for us to express our joy and to show our love to all.

"And we are happier than you think to be part of it all; and we are happy to see you are doing this for us, and it will be in print too!

"We would like to express our gratitude to you and we would like to say this is a great way for people to see all we do for them, and show them how we help them.

"My friends are here too, and we watch over your house and we are watching over many others. And this is the way we thank people for doing good works for our Father, who loves all and sees all and who wants all of you to be home with us in the long run.

"We will say a few words each and it will suffice for now. And this will be the beginning of a marvelous friendship with all the people who want to say hello to us, too.

"We are here for you and we always will be! Goodbye for now and we will see you here with us, in the future."

"Goodbye Gabriel; thank you for calling in so unexpectedly."

"And goodbye too Lee, it is my pleasure to speak to you today!"

House of Cherubim

Guardian angels residing in this house look after those born
- 1st May to 10th June -

God says, "Angels residing in this house are my special purpose workers who escort me in my travels and help me in my daily endeavors. These angels are always helping me keep records and guarding my house."

HAZIEL -   looks after those born on 1st May to 5th May.

"Lee it is Haziel!"

"Hello Haziel, are you an angel from the House of Cherubim?"

"Lee, I am the angel Haziel who is from the House of Cherubim and I send messages to the people on earth telling them when they are going to have children. I let them have children as I am the one who provides them with their fertility and I give them the urge to procreate.

"I will be the one who decides on the gender and I will tell the parents what they are getting if they ask me as I can tell those who ask.

"Few ever ask and I can show them what their child will look like if they ask, but they never ask. I can show them what the child will do for a living if they ask, but they never ask; so I go on doing my work regardless of whether they ask or not, as I love doing my work.

"I love helping out those who want children if they ask, and some ask but others just forget to, and nothing happens for them!"

"Thanks Haziel, would you like to tell me about anything else?"

"Lee, I am also the angel who gives help to the charioteers carrying God's throne and I escort Him with His entourage wherever he goes."

Chapter 2. House of Cherubim.

"And I am so proud to be part of the parade that sometimes I forget to tell people about the pending births of their children, so they are surprised, to say the least."

"Forget? Yes Haziel, I actually do remember seeing a woman on television recently who had just given birth and she said that she had been unaware of being pregnant."

"Lee, she was an oversight and I was to blame. Our Father said to keep an eye out and delegate more of my duties to my helpers in future. I need to go look now, so goodbye."

"Thanks Haziel, I'll look forward to speaking to you again soon, goodbye."

ALADIAH -   looks after those born on 6th May to 10th May.

"Lee, it is Aladiah!"

"Are you Aladiah, an angel from the House of Cherubim?"

"Lee, it is, and I am; and I can give you the details you want as I have been waiting for you to ask me, and here you are as promised.

"So let us get some of my details down for the readers as I have a lot of good things to say, and I love telling people good things as it is good for them and negates all the bad vibes they have.

"Let me tell them firstly that after death there is another existence that is a better reality than the illusion of reality they live in at the moment. Even though the world is solid and they hurt physically and feel emotion, the real world is here where all things are known. I can tell you that they are going to be in for a surprise, as I am the angel who has to tell them where they are, on the spiritual scale of reality; and I can make their lives so good, they couldn't even begin to guess at how good! Let me explain about the way they speak to each other too, as the least little amount of

Chapter 2. House of Cherubim.

thought can be picked up and even the smallest amount of love they feel will be transferred to the recipient as well as any others who are in the path, and many, many feelings are picked up. Try to be more positive and loving so that we can bask in the joy of the feelings people express for each other and try to block out the negativity. But some inadvertently creeps in, so try to be more positive in your outlook too."

"Aladiah, would you like to say anything else?"

"Yes Lee, I am an angel of the Lord who does His personal waiting and I am the one who tells the others waiting for His news, the news they are waiting to hear as I know it in advance. And I give them a prelude to the incoming messages – as I am a messenger first and foremost.

"My duties entail being here to pass any messages on that Father has for the others who wait and I also give messages to people who are receptive to them; and the messages are usually of a good nature as I do not convey bad news, only good news."

"Thanks Aladiah, goodbye for now."

LAUVIAH -   looks after those born on 11th May to 15th May.

"Hello, Lee it is Lauviah."

"Are you Lauviah, an angel from the House of Cherubim?"

"Yes Lee, I am Lauviah, also an angel of the Lord."

"Lauviah, can you give me a brief rundown of your duties and also a few comments about yourself?"

"Lee, yes I can. I would like to say plenty about the way the world is going if you want to hear it. And I can tell you it is not all good for now so we had better pull our socks up or things will get out of hand. And the world leaders need pulling up too as they are irresponsible fools."

Chapter 2. House of Cherubim.

"I would like to say that when the time comes for us to judge them they will rue the day they were ever born. And they will be punished; and I will be just as delighted as the rest of the long suffering world.

"We are all in this world to be here for each other and most forget that they are supposed to help one another and continue to go about their daily lives without so much as a thought for the ones left without food or shelter. I am the angel who looks out for those seeking food and shelter, and all that pray get assistance as there are many... far too many. And the Western World is to blame for this as they are taking unfair advantage of the underprivileged and exploiting them as well as using their resources.

"I am ready to put an end to this as soon as the time is right and I will put a stop to it as I see fit, as our Father has authorized me to do so. My brethren are going to be busy escorting all those who have not gained a position in the light to the end that awaits them and they will be punished for their actions."

"Lauviah, would you like to add any more to what you have said so far?"

"Yes Lee, I would like to say that the next book you are going to write will be about Father's new rules. This will be a shock for most people as they have been led up the garden path as you already know. You had better be careful about who you let see this work as you may bear the brunt of their hateful jibes for giving them '*The Word*' as you are going to be told.[4] So be prepared for this, as I would not like to see you come under attack for doing good works for our Father and not be rewarded for your efforts - as it is a major shake up. And most will be smarting, and most will be in disbelief; and all will be shaking, as '*The Word*' has a

---

[4] See (Revelation 10:7-10)

Chapter 2. House of Cherubim.

lot of information about their future. And all will wonder at '*The Word*,' and all will be astonished at the depth of information; and most will be lost, as you know."

"Yes Lauviah, we will leave it there for now if you don't mind and thanks for your comments; goodbye, my friend."

HAHAIAH -   looks after those born on 16th May to 20th May.

"Are you there, Hahaiah?"

"Lee it is Hahaiah, an angel of the Lord."

"Are you Hahaiah from the House of Cherubim?"

"Yes Lee, and I am the angel who goes everywhere with our Father and I watch all that is happening. I oversee the finer details of the travel plans He has and so we look out for whatever needs to be done. And we assign the work to whoever has responsibility for that task, and we all try to be up front in whatever we do, as you know.

"My main duties entail keeping track of all of our Father's acquaintances and whoever He needs to contact at any given moment for any given task, as I would not be able to delegate all of it. So I have to have helpers, but usually it is sufficient with the number of other angels who are prepared to stop what they are doing to lend a hand."

"Would you like to add any more to that, Hahaiah?"

"Yes Lee, I will let you know what I do when my duties are done and there is a spare minute as we do not sleep or eat, nor do we have much time for any type of recreation. We will always be busy doing our work until the day of the resurrection when all will cease and all these duties will end. I have the opportunity to visit and speak to my friends who are in the other realms and sometimes I also speak to the human beings

Chapter 2. House of Cherubim.

who are my Father's messengers on earth, such as you and Golaiah, along with a few others."

"I will be contacting Golaiah shortly as I want to meet her in her present form, as I have not had the pleasure yet. It will be a moment for me to remember as she will be in charge of the nine celestial houses at the time of judgment. So when the time comes she will be in the position of delegating our duties, until all is over.

"Then we can rest and have our time together, sharing stories and reminiscing over all the centuries we have known each other.[5] It will be a time of great joy for me and it will be a great time for the other angels too, as we are all looking forward to this. And it will mean that we have completed our duties."

"Yes, Hahaiah - and it will be a time of great jubilation and rejoicing for all the faithful believers too."

"Yes, that is correct and I would like to thank you for the opportunity of saying these few words here with you today; goodbye Lee, I will go now, goodbye."

"Thank you for being here with me today, Hahaiah, goodbye."

---

[5] The Day of Judgment will span over a period of one thousand years. Where Hahaiah speaks about, '...reminiscing over all the centuries we have known each other' he means both the memories from previous times in the spiritual realms that will be restored to me and to Golaiah from our past-lives, as well as the times he envisages in the future one thousand years that we will spend together.

Golaiah and I can both access our past-life records either by personally examining the Angelic Records, by asking our guardian angels for the information or by channeling our higher-selves. For most people though, past-life records will only be available to them in spirit, as the living brain supplied with each new incarnation has no prior memories, being fresh. The brain only takes in and stores information about the life it is living in at the moment.

All past-life memories will be fully restored to the soul at the time of judgment.

Chapter 2. House of Cherubim.

IEZALEL - looks after those born on 21st May to 25th May.

"Hello Iezalel, may I speak to you for a few minutes?"

"Lee it is Iezalel!"

"Are you Iezalel, an angel from the House of Cherubim?"

"Yes I am Lee; do you want me to tell you what I do during my time and what I do not do, or just what I am supposed to do?"

"Iezalel, we would like to know what you actually do, and if you have time, to give us a few beneficial words about yourself."

"Lee, we all have different duties and we help each other in times of need; and we try to get all of the work done as it is getting more each day, and we have been extremely busy up till now.

"I am the angel who speaks to those souls in spirit wanting help in matters pertaining to their immediate past-lives as some have problems that still need resolving. And they are restless as they cannot come to grips with the way things have turned out for them.

"And I give them the opportunity to go over these times with me and we look at what could have happened; and they see the difference if other paths had been taken. Some are glad that they did what they did whilst others wish they had followed a different path.

"I give them hope for a brighter future and counsel them in the light of hindsight, as it is all written down so they can learn from their mistakes and grow. The ones who have had more lives are old souls and are wiser, therefore the spirits are a mixture of young and silly and old and wise souls; so the mix makes for an interesting combination of all types.

"They are all different races too as we have given human beings many choices of who they can be in the world, as some have to be rich and some have to be poor, as it would be boring if all were the same in each life. So the lives are variable giving a rich experience overall that can be

Chapter 2. House of Cherubim.

looked back on with reflection, to learn from; and this is the reason... this is the reason really, that people have so many lives.

"I am giving you this as it will be interesting for the people to read and will allow them to understand how we operate here in the light and why they have the chance of life. It is all arranged from here, as they, as an entity are given a new born body to enter into if they want to reincarnate again. And they usually do as the excitement is too much, being able to physically touch each other once again, as they cannot here. And to have that experience is worth all the pain and suffering in the end."

"Iezalel, can angels physically touch humans?"

"Yes Lee, and this is a problem that caused much concern in the years long ago when they mated with their human counterparts. And our Father created a flood to wipe their offspring out due to this. He was annoyed with us allowing our brethren to do this and this led to a falling out of many and also an ongoing feud that has not been resolved yet."

"What happened to these angels, Iezalel?"

"They have fallen from grace in the sight of God and they are banished from their house in heaven. And this house remains empty, and this house is barren; and this house has not been heard of since, as it has been out of bounds to all of us; and this house is the House of Nephilim.

"And all of the Nephilim are now on the earth plane and they are waiting to be judged too. And these angels are waiting with the evil ones, and they are reduced in power and rank and have no favor in Father's eyes or in His house anymore."

"That's very interesting Iezalel, thank you and goodbye for now."

"Goodbye Lee, I will be here anytime you want to contact me."

Chapter 2. House of Cherubim.

MEBAHEL - looks after those born on 26th May to 31st May.

"Lee, it is Mebahel!"

"Are you Mebahel, an angel from the House of Cherubim?"

"Yes I am and I want to say that you are a good man and I want to say that we are all watching over you and Golaiah at the moment. We are expecting a lot from both of you as you progress and it will be wonderful to see the difference it makes in the world once you are both on the way.

"So please tell all your readers that we are going to be here doing our work regardless of what is happening, and not to be downhearted; but instead think about the times ahead when life will be wonderful for all those remaining, without crime or any form of sin!"

"So you're telling me that Golaiah and I will both have specific roles to play in the future, Mebahel?"

"Yes, Lee, and I will be happy when it begins to happen as we have waited long enough already."

"Would you like to tell me about yourself, Mebahel?"

"Lee, I go about my duties as the messenger telling people to keep their money in the bank as the system looks like falling to pieces shortly, and they will be caught short if they are investing as the world economy is going to slump. There will be a lot of people going without soon... so my job is to help those who ask and guide them to find the best answer in each case, as the amount of people going to need assistance will be enormous."

"Would you like to add any further comments, Mebahel?"

"Yes, I will add a few more comments and that is to say, keep going as you are and do not worry, as our Father is helping. You are going to be alright and you will be able to help others who need it."

"Okay, Mebahel, thank you for your insights and encouragement."

Chapter 2. House of Cherubim.

"Lee, do you want any more information?"

"By all means Mebahel, feel free to speak."

"I am giving help to some people who run the economy and know what is happening. So if you watch the television you will see a decline in spending as public confidence is starting to drop and shortly you will see a downturn in small business. This glitch will go on until next year now and we will see many conflicts, so - be warned. Also keep out of the firing line yourself and do not get involved, as it may come home to roost."

"Thanks Mebahel; I will be an onlooker only, not a participant; so do not worry my friend! Thanks again and goodbye for now."

"Goodbye Lee, please come back and talk about this later."

"Okay I will, thanks for your time."

HARIEL - looks after those born on 1st June to 5th June.

"Hello Hariel, have you got a spare minute?"

"Lee? Yes it is me, Hariel!"

"Are you Hariel, an angel from the House of Cherubim?"

"Yes I am, and what can I do for you?"

"I would like a brief duty statement and a few comments about your personal life, please."

"Lee, okay, I will give you a brief statement outlining my duties and also a little about my personal side; what do you want to know?"

"Hariel, I would like to know how you spend your time in the heavenly realms and what you do there."

"I look after the people who are in pain and I alleviate their pain by merging their consciousness into the spiritual realms. I take them on a journey to take the pain away from them, and it is as if they have an out

Chapter 2. House of Cherubim.

of body experience until their body is able to cope with it. Then I take them back into their bodies to take over the basic functions again; and the heart is started in some, and the kidneys; liver and lungs start functioning again, so they survive the experience."

"Hariel, do you mean to say this is like an NDE?" [6]

"Yes, it is a near death experience for some, as not all leave their bodies when they are in great pain because the threshold of pain differs for each individual. Some leave very quickly, whereas others hang on grimly until a blanket of darkness overcomes them and forces them out of their body, to let it go until it can cope again.

"And if it cannot cope they come with me, and I introduce them to their spirit guides; and they hover around until it can be determined whether to return to their body, or to remain in spirit."

"Hariel, what happens to those who aren't worthy of going to the light and have to remain on the earth plane?"

"I give them the opportunity to go back into their body, the same as anybody else; and if they refuse to return, I check their records then call their spirit guides. And their soul is then escorted back to the earth plane, to the waiting room known as hell - and they remain there in spirit."

"That's interesting, Hariel. Where do most souls go who wish to remain in the spirit world, I mean, which level do most end up on?"

"Lee, the majority of dead - or their souls, end up left on the earth plane as most have not earned the right to be allowed into the light."

"What about those spirit mediums that contact these unworthy souls left on the earth plane, and think they're rescuing them by telling them to go to the light?"

---

[6] Near death experience.

Chapter 2. House of Cherubim.

"That is impossible as they cannot go to the light unless they have been forgiven and it has been approved by the proper authority. This is the same as asking you to fly to Mars without a space ship, or to enter into the Kingdom of God before the Day of Judgment."

"I see! Then a lot of people working as spirit mediums are misguided then?"

"Yes, they have no right to interfere with the spirit world as this is for those who are authorized by God! They are not really accomplishing anything at all as the spirits they tell to go to the light cannot go and then become even unhappier than they were before!"

"Is it possible then for deceased souls who are left on the earth plane to go to the light?"

"Yes Lee, if they are truly sorry for their misdeeds and ask an angel or a proper authorized messenger to pray for them to be forgiven,[7] then our Father will hear them and decide whether or not to allow them into the light.

"All others will be judged on their merits on the Day of Judgment and those who do not go to the light at that time will be punished and will either remain there to reflect on their actions or relive and feel all the pain they have inflicted on others, before they perish."

---

[7] Souls who are left on the earth plane cannot pray to be forgiven as they are not heard by God. They need a living person or a messenger to do this for them on or before the Day of Judgment. Lost souls are different again. These souls may be eligible to enter the light but remain on the earth plane either to resolve unfinished business or because of a traumatic event they need to see redressed.

These disturbed souls sometimes manifest as ghosts and only they can be guided to the light by spirit mediums that have attained at least the level of introduction in the spiritual realms, and work in this area.

Chapter 2. House of Cherubim.

"That seems to be a bit harsh, for a kind and loving God to inflict this sort of punishment on these sinners, Hariel."

"Lee! How can you say that? Our Father is kind to those He loves, but woe betide those who lose favor in His eyes as He will not have them in His house and He discards them! This is to get rid of those who would pollute the earth and to get rid of those with bad thoughts who would do evil things if they ever got another opportunity again!"

"Hariel, what do you do in your own personal time?"

"My time is taken up by looking into the lives of lost souls left on the earth plane and putting things into perspective for them, alleviating their misery by guiding their spirit guides to people who were directly involved in their case; and I try to direct the proceedings so that all is resolved, then the guides can find people to report those details to, to those who need them, to pray for them, and then those souls are free to come to the light unencumbered."

"Thanks Hariel, we had better leave it there as I have some more angels to interview shortly. Thank you very much for the information as some readers may not have known this, and this is the reason I have asked you to explain it."

"Lee, I thought so as you know how we operate here and I know that some will read this and learn what they did not know before; farewell."

"Thank you Hariel, goodbye for now."

God says, "Lost souls are allowed to enter into the light if they are entitled to, and they are the only exception. These souls will not usually let go of the earth plane if they are still trying to resolve a major problem."

"Thank you, Father."

Chapter 2. House of Cherubim.

HEKAMIAH - looks after those born on 6th June to 10th June.

"Hekamiah, are you there?"

"Lee, it is Hekamiah!"

"Hello Hekamiah, are you an angel from the House of Cherubim?"

"Yes, it is Hekamiah from the Cherubim. You have been asking all the others in this house a lot of questions and it is now my turn to speak."

"Yes Hekamiah, and I'd like you to tell me what your duties are and then ask you to give me a few comments about yourself, if I may?"

"Lee, I do many things and one of my primary duties is to look after the women on earth who are not married, as I have the role to help them in their choice of men. The spirit guides who are helping them in their daily lives ask me for advice about the men they are involved with as I can check their angelic records to see if they are the right one for them."

"Well Hekamiah, why is it that so many men and women choose the wrong partner and their marriage ends up in divorce?"

"Lee, it is not a matter of choosing the wrong partner for most... it is compromise that saves the day in the long run. These men and women who are unhappy have to examine their reasons closely before making the final decision to leave home, or to break off with their partner and divorce them."

"But not all would agree with what you are saying here about people getting divorced, Hekamiah, due to their religious beliefs."

"Lee, I help those who ask and as for the others I do not know of the difficulties they face, only helping my flock and I keep my eye on them to ensure all is going well."

"Tell me then Hekamiah, what happens if you approve of a man and a woman being together, then things turn sour, say alcohol abuse or physical violence erupts?"

Chapter 2. House of Cherubim.

"Yes it happens and then we send recommendations for that man or woman to remove him or herself from the situation if possible. And if it is not possible we send the man's or the woman's spirit guides to influence them, trying to get him or her to see the wrong they are doing."

"What happens if they do not listen to their spirit guides, Hekamiah?"

"It can be difficult for all concerned as the man or woman can be addicted to drink or drugs and may have psychological problems to overcome, so we try to bring them to the attention of a professional person who can help."

"Hekamiah, what about the rules some religions impose on divorce?"

"A good question and the answer is that to remain in a bad situation is unwise and to leave is best as to remain could end up in tragedy. The emotional pain is bad enough without the final result being made worse by leaving yourself in a vulnerable position.

"And where the Bible says, 'No person must separate what God has joined together',[8] Jesus meant that no person should interfere in or break up a happy marriage, not meaning it for those or relating to those in disharmony and conflict with each other as this is not His way. And the people who are happy in their marriage have me to thank as it is my duty to help - and if it looks promising at the start, then their guides go ahead and say so."

"Would you like to give me a little insight into your personal life now, please Hekamiah?"

"Yes, alright Lee; the way I relax is to have my friends around discussing the issues and we enjoy talking about what has already transpired and what is going to happen next."

"So you are saying that you can tell the future, Hekamiah?"

---

[8] See (Matthew 19:6)

Chapter 2. House of Cherubim.

"No, what I am saying is that we put all the facts we have in front of us and then draw the most likely conclusions from the evidence at hand."

"So you cannot tell of future events?"

"No we cannot; only our Father can see in advance what will happen as all people have free will and people can change their minds and do whatever they like; so there really is not much we can tell about future events in the lives of people with any certainty."

"Hekamiah, you are able to read minds as all those in the spirit world can, so you should be able to see what people intend to do in the future, shouldn't you?"

"Yes we can read minds and know the person's most intimate innermost thoughts and we base our decisions on this information, but as you know a person can change his or her mind and do irrational things. And most people do not carry out many of the thoughts on their mind, anyway."

"So how do some of these fortunetellers come up with the correct answers then, Hekamiah?"

"They look at the possibilities open to that person by asking the person's guides and they go with the most likely foreseeable outcome. The fortunetellers can provide a fair indication from this information, but it really is all left to chance."

"Well thank you for your input Hekamiah, I'll speak to you again as soon as I get some free time."

"Lee, I have enjoyed your company and I too would like to meet you again for a more detailed discussion as this is more general information, rather than spiritual enlightenment we are giving you at the moment - as you can tell. I am already looking forward to our next personal meeting."

"Thanks Hekamiah, I'll look forward to that too; goodbye for now."

"Lee, it has been a wonderful discussion, thank you; goodbye."

House of Thrones

Guardian angels residing in this house look after those born
- 11th June to 22nd July -

God says, "The angels in my House of Thrones look after the people who bring universal justice to the land and let the unspoken rules and regulations manifest as best they can."

LAHUIAH - looks after those born on 11th June to 15th June.

"Lee, it is Lahuiah!"

"Hello Lahuiah, are you an angel from the House of Thrones?"

"Yes I am and I am the angel who instructs the living in matters of religion and also in matters regarding the moral values they have. It is my duty to inform them of their moral obligations to each other and I give out instructions for them to carry on their conscience.

"Many listen to me but many do not, so they are not able to follow my wisdom and therefore will suffer the consequences. All are given the information and all have an inner voice telling them right from wrong. All know whether they are doing good or not and all have the choice to do good or evil. And the end result of following the wrong path is eternal hell or even worse."

"So what exactly is eternal hell, Lahuiah? Are you able to describe this?"

"Yes Lee, it means the souls of the dead who have not made the grade are left on the earth plane to suffer and they are left without their senses except for communication by thought. They are left to dwell on their past sins until our Father passes further judgment on them. Then

Chapter 3. House of Thrones.

they will either die the second death, remain to suffer, or be promoted to the light at the time of judgment."

"Is the second death what you meant when you said, '...or even worse,' Lahuiah?"

"Of course it is and the ones who are forgiven have only sinned in a small way so they are redeemed, and then they are free to go on, on to another life or to remain in the light as they wish.

"But the ones who remain in the light are usually asked to be guides for the living and to look after specific people with specific needs, as this is a way to get up the ladder here. Then the level they finally reach will be more rewarding for them when the last days are here, as then no-one can be changed from one realm to another as it is the final judgment."

"Thank you Lahuiah, and now, can you tell me a few things about yourself?"

"Okay Lee, but my life is my work, so the following words are all about me and about my work. I do whatever Father asks me to do without question and efficiently as His decision is final.

"And I do a lot of personal work intervening with people who may die in accidents or may die by some other means, and I stop this as Father instructs me to do so."

"What determines whether you save one life and let another go, Lahuiah?"

"Lee, it depends on the situation at hand, as sometimes we try to save people where it is impossible; such as in a horrific car smash in which the body is damaged too much, or a fall from a building and the brain is damaged too much; or anything that we cannot help such as the plane being directed into the World Trade Center, or any act made by human decision; as people have free will to do whatever they like. And we try to keep tabs on all of it but it is a losing battle at the moment."

Chapter 3. House of Thrones.

"So what does God say when you cannot save someone He has asked you to?"

"Lee, it saddens Him and He becomes very quiet for a few minutes. Then He resumes by giving further instructions without stopping again, as He needs to keep going at all times as He can think of millions of things at once. Father listens to all things and sees all things and is present in all things, as He permeates into everything and is part of all living and non-living matter.

"Father has mysterious ways of doing things that are impossible to tell others about as none of us are able to describe what we see and no-one knows what He can do or cannot do in the heavens, as all His work stems from original thought."

"Well thank you very much, Lahuiah, I'm sure the people will be interested in reading what you have told me, and I'll leave it there for now."

"Goodbye Lee, and please get back to me as soon as you can as I need to speak to you about many other issues, and you are the one who may be able to help."

"Okay, Lahuiah, I'll speak to you again later on; goodbye."

CALIEL - looks after those born on 11th June to 15th June.

"Hello Caliel, may I speak to you?"

"Lee it is Caliel; what do you want to ask me about?"

"Are you Caliel, an angel from the House of Thrones?"

"Yes I am, and I will tell you a little bit about myself if that is what I am here for."

"Yes, it is why you're here Caliel, and I'd like to ask you about your heavenly duties and a little about your private life too."

Chapter 3. House of Thrones.

"Lee, it is not a very exciting life but we like what we do and if the people would like to read about it, then they can, but as I said it is not exactly an electrifying story."

"Firstly, Caliel, do you spell your name 'Caliel' as it appears in the heading?"

"I always spell it with an 'aitch' as Cahliel so do it as you wish but I prefer it as I spell it. It has been a few weeks since you called me and you have been unwell and you have been doing my Father's work, have you not?"

"True, Cahliel, I have started auto-typing His book though have been a little off color lately, but I'm feeling a little better now thanks."

"Lee, if you like I can send some healing to you and it will make your illness go away as we can alleviate this if you ask for it, as a lot of people get healed by asking for healing. A lot of people can now see and a lot of people can now walk after being confined to a wheelchair. And a lot of people are able to lead normal lives after being healed with the power of the Holy Spirit which enters into them and heals them, as they are believers in the power of our Father.

"They pray to Him for healing and He provides people with healing hands to go out among the people to heal them. Our Father provides the sick and the dying with all types of helpers who are there for them if they ask. Our Father wants people to be healthy and not bound in bandages or be in poor health. The spirit of blindness and the spirit of deafness are cast out of a lot of people who are blind and who are deaf and who suffer maladies which bear no name and which have no medicine to cure, and He provides these to those who ask.

"And all who ask in good faith in the belief of being cured will be, and all who do not believe will not be. It depends on the faith of the person, as they are the one's receiving the Holy Spirit. And the Holy Spirit cannot

Chapter 3. House of Thrones.

or will not enter those who are not ready, as the Holy Spirit is from our Father. And our Father gives this to His flock and they are His children, and His children are those who believe in Him."

"Thanks Cahliel, I recall reading somewhere in the Bible about people being cured like this."

"Lee, I will give you a sample of the power of this healing power right now, if you like?"

"Right now, Cahliel?"

"Yes, yesterday you had blurry vision didn't you, and your blood pressure was high too, wasn't it?"

"Yes, that's true and it's still high; so what are you going to do?"

"If you check in an hour's time your blood pressure will be back to normal and your blurry vision will be better too!"

"Okay! Thanks Cahliel, I should soon be feeling much better then."

"Can you tell me anything about your personal life, Cahliel?"

"Lee of course; if you think my story is worthy I can tell you something about myself, as it is a part of me. And if you need to know more, the house is open to you as you know, and you may look at the written records. If you recall, the Second World War had many casualties. Well, I was the one who helped millions recover from wounds which would normally have taken months to recover from, and I gave them healing as they asked for it and they recovered much, much faster than they could possibly have done without my help. And this is why some take longer to heal than others, as they are unable to get my help without my Father's permission, as He hears their prayers and then sends me to help."

"Thank you for your story, Cahliel and for the alternative way of spelling your name."

"Lee, I would like to speak to you again soon, as I want to know the answers to a few things that you can help me with."

Chapter 3. House of Thrones.

"Cahliel, I thought you could read people's minds and find out all their thoughts."

"That's true Lee, but I can only read your immediate thoughts; your innermost thoughts are inaccessible at the moment as you are surrounded by Father's protective white light which blocks all others from reading your mind, unless you are conversing with them for purposes of communication. But truly, I am telling you, at the moment I cannot read your innermost thoughts."

"Okay, Cahliel; I'll speak to you again later when I get a spare minute; goodbye for now!"

"Goodbye Lee."

LEUVIAH -   looks after those born on 22nd June to 26th June.

"Hello Leuviah, may I speak to you?"

"Lee it is Leuviah!"

"Are you Leuviah, the guardian angel from the House of Thrones?"

"Lee it is! It is very good to hear from you as I have been waiting to meet you."

"Leuviah, would you like to tell me about the main duties you carry out and if you have time, let me know what you do in your own free time?"

"Lee, I am the angel who provides the crops and the cattle for the people. I look after the distribution of the food supplies and I try to oversee that the foods are distributed fairly. But at the moment the wealthier countries keep most of it and do not let the other poorer countries have enough to feed their populations, as it is not economical for them to transport it and sell it to them at a lower price.

"The governments need to learn that people are more important than the economy and to let the poor have a share of the leftovers."

Chapter 3. House of Thrones.

"What do you do in your spare time, Leuviah?"

"Lee, my spare time is spent trying to persuade the world leaders to distribute food and provide other life saving sustenance to poorer countries by giving Foreign Aid, and I have succeeded to a certain extent by pricking their consciences. But it is not enough yet and eventually we will be able to provide food for all when the Day of Judgment is upon us, for then Father's messengers will oversee the distribution of food to all."

"Thank you for the information Leuviah, goodbye for now."

"Goodbye Lee, it has been a pleasure to speak to you; and I will contact you again shortly."

PAHALIAH - looks after those born on 27th June to 1st July.

"Pahaliah, may I speak to you for a few minutes?"
"Lee, it is Pahaliah!"
"Are you Pahaliah, an angel from the House of Thrones?"

"Lee, yes I am and I am here to tell you of my duties and to tell you about my personal life, and I will try to give you the details as I remember them.

"I am the angel who gives people the incentive to go and learn as much as they can, as they are better equipped to do more good if they are educated. And this gives them a good start to earn their bread and butter.

"And they learn that the air is made from different gases, and the birds of the air are made from different gases; and that I am made from the gases as they are made from the gases.

"The bones in their bodies are all counted and are made from the gases, and all matter is made from the gases."

Chapter 3. House of Thrones.

"So all is made from the gases; and they are wise when they know this, and they are knowledgeable when they know this.

"And they are able to tell each other about their newfound wisdom, and they are made to feel important with their newfound knowledge; and they are able to go out into the world with confidence, feeling important.

"God is part of the gases that they are made from, and He is part of them and they are part of Him. Therefore they are made in His likeness, as the gases are made from atoms and the atoms are all about us and within us and abound about us; therefore, we are all made from the gases."

"Thank you, Pahaliah and now would you like to give me a few details about your personal life in heaven?"

"Lee, I would; and I give plenty of my time to all who ask, and my personal time is made up of visiting people and watching over them; seeing that they are going to be alright and offering them insights into their future work, as I can direct them toward the field that they would be best suited to."

"Is this how you spend all of your spare time, Pahaliah?"

"Yes Lee, it is always a pleasure for me to do this and when people learn that helping others is more rewarding than the personal pursuits they follow, this world will be a better place; and soon it will be, as the angels are preparing for a big event soon and this event will be the start of a new era. Actually, I am being called right now to help someone in need! I will return straight after this mission is over if you still need me; goodbye."

"Goodbye, Pahaliah; thank you for your interesting contribution."

Chapter 3. House of Thrones.

NELCHAEL - looks after people born on 2nd July to 6th July.

"Hello Nelchael, are you free for a few minutes?"

"Lee, it is Nelchael and yes, I can spare some of my time for you."

"Are you Nelchael, an angel from the House of Thrones?"

"Yes Lee, I am and I do God's work and I am proud of doing this work."

"Can you tell me what you do and also give me an insight into your private life?"

"Lee, I visit the terminally ill before they cross over and introduce them to their spirit guides who escort them to the spiritual level they have attained during the course of their life."

"Well Nelchael, that would make them feel a whole lot better about dying as they would then realize that they're going to survive after death, and that death isn't the end after all."

"That's right Lee, as some are led to believe that death is the end and they are conscious of nothing at all - as Solomon declared in his wisdom without the true spiritual understanding of what he was saying." [9]

"So what happens when you arrive and they see you, Nelchael?"

"Lee, they are usually greatly relieved and overjoyed as they are normally frightened of dying and the thought of leaving their loved ones behind, thinking they are never going to see them again."

"Yes that's understandable; I have also heard that the dead are conscious of nothing at all; so why are people being told this if it is not true?"

"Lee, it was written in the scriptures by King Solomon who held this opinion and it has misled many people; but now, because Judgment Day

---

[9] See (Ecclesiastes 9:5)

Chapter 3. House of Thrones.

is not far off, we are letting all know that they do survive after death, and are even more aware of everything than the living."

"Well I guess that will be very good news for most people who think that they are not going to be conscious of anything at all after death, or at least until the resurrection."

"Lee, it is good news... yes, many will find it difficult to believe, but they will eventually find out the truth."

"Thank you Nelchael, this has been interesting and I guess some of our readers will think so too."

"Lee, the information should be told to everyone, not just our readers and I will work out a way to do this later on."

"Nelchael, can you give me some idea of what you do in your own personal time?"

"Lee, I do many things and the main pastime I have is to go and visit my friends who are still living on earth as they are usually people I have been watching over in times of trouble, and they have asked God to help them. And I keep watching over them as I feel they are good people, and I try to help them as much as possible."

"Okay thanks, Nelchael; goodbye for now my friend."

YEIAYEL - looks after those born on 7th July to 11th July.

"Hello Yeiayel, may I speak to you?"

"Lee? Do you want to interview me now?"

"Yes Yeiayel; are you the angel Yeiayel from the House of Thrones?"

"Lee, it is Yeiayel and I am from the House of Thrones; are you going to ask me what I do in the house now?"

"Yes, if you have time; would you mind?"

"Of course not; so what is the reason for this?"

Chapter 3. House of Thrones.

"Yeiayel, I want to add your comments to a list that I am making of guardian angels roles and the duties they carry out, for any people who may be interested. The other angels have been discussing it between themselves."

"Lee, I have heard the others speaking about it, but I want to know why you are letting all the people see this as it is not known by any other living human being. I am wondering if they should know these things about us as they argue incessantly, and they will argue about this as they argue about all things. This makes them think about things as they have many unresolved issues and it is a way to let off steam, arguing!

"They need a set of beliefs and a football team to cheer and they need a political party to vote for. And they need to go to the beach as others do, and they need to buy lottery tickets as others do; and they need to eat in restaurants as others do and drink sparkling wines as others do, to be a part of the team."

"Yes Yeiayel, there's no denying that people argue and need plenty of leisurely activities to occupy themselves with, but that's how they are and they can choose to read what you have to say or discard it as they see fit. It's up to the individual person to find out what you do, and if they're interested, then reading this will be a way for them to do that. Would you like to give me some idea of the duties you carry out in the heavenly realms?"

"Lee, I do many things and my main duty is on the physical earth keeping the animals happy as they are important to me. I keep them calm and tell them to behave, and I soothe their fears and help them when they give birth in the wilds. I kill the ones that are too ill to look after themselves anymore. And I take the animals into the wilderness to survive the encroachment of humans, and try to keep them safe from poachers. These are the things I do!"

Chapter 3. House of Thrones.

"Thank you Yeiayel, now can you also give me some details about your personal life, such as what you do when you have some spare time to yourself?"

"Lee, of course - I can tell you the answer to that as it seems important to you, but is it?"

"Yes it is Yeiayel, as we would like to have an understanding of what goes on in the heavenly realms, as none of us living right now have been told about it yet, or what it's like to be there."

"Lee, then I will tell you this; I spend my spare time watching over my animal friends to save them from fires and tell them where the water holes are, and where to get food. And I give them the directions they need to go from one place to another, so you see, my spare time is spent with the animals of the earth; and I spend most of my time here and rarely visit my home where I reside, as I prefer to be here."

"Thanks Yeiayel, now, just one more question, if I may? What would you be doing if you were at home in heaven and weren't here on earth looking after the animals?"

"I would be playing with my trumpets and playing my stringed instruments which we do from time to time. I also love to participate in the grand concerts we have and I would love to be singing the hymns that are sung daily. And I would love to walk through the beautiful gardens that we have and view the magnificent cathedrals that are there; and the wonders that are there are marvelous to behold!"

"Well Yeiayel, it sounds very good to me; everybody will be just dying to get in."

"Lee, you jest?"

"Yes, it was said with tongue in cheek. I hope I haven't offended you, as I didn't mean to."

Chapter 3. House of Thrones.

"No, I laughed at your silly joke; do not worry, I have a sense of humor too."

"Thank you for your time Yeiayel; hopefully we'll have another chat later on; goodbye for now."

"Lee, goodbye and I hope your readers will believe me, as I know people!"

MELAHEL - looks after those born on 12th July to 16th July.

"Hello Melahel, do you have any spare time free at the moment, for an interview with me?"

"Lee, it is Melahel!"

"Are you Melahel an angel from the House of Thrones?"

"Yes I am and I am from the House of Thrones!"

"Would you like to tell me what you do in the house and what your main duties are, Melahel?"

"I am the angel who guards the entrance to the house. And I am on guard duty day and night for weeks at a time until I am relieved from this, to look after those on earth who call for help, and then I respond to the call!"

"What sort of work do you do when you are called, Melahel?"

"I am the one who escorts the children to the light, the ones who die at birth or are killed at the time of their birth, mainly by lethal injection in some eastern countries to keep the population down."

"Okay! Well that *is* sad, and what else do you do?"

"The amount of children dying is staggering Lee; all over the world they die like flies every day in the thousands from disease, starvation and euthanasia. And I am going full time to keep up with it even though

Chapter 3. House of Thrones.

Father now lets me have as many helpers as I need to do this, due to the workload, until I am sent back on guard duty for a break."

"What do you do when you have spare time to yourself, Melahel?"

"Lee, it is a time for me to forget my duties and I relax, playing the flute, listening to the birds singing and listening to the insects humming. And I look at all the beautiful things Father has provided in nature and rejoice in these, as I have the knowledge that all things will be much better after the Day of Judgment, and these wicked events will no longer take place."

"Melahel, I hope this Day of Judgment is not too far away, as the way people treat each other today is beyond belief. Thank you for your comments, goodbye for now."

"Goodbye Lee, I hope the people reading this are horrified at the truths they see here!"

HAHUIAH - looks after those born on 17th July to 22nd July.

"Hello Hahuiah, may I speak to you for a few minutes?"

"Lee, it is Hahuiah!"

"Are you Hahuiah, an angel from the House of Thrones?"

"Yes Lee, and how are you?"

"I'm fine thanks; right now I'm gathering information on guardian angels to give to people, so I've decided to ask each of you about your role and a little personal information about yourself."

"Lee, we know and we are happy to tell you, and we are pleased that you are doing this as our Father is happy with it.

"We would like you to tell all the people about our work and the kingdom of heaven, as not many believe it is true."

Chapter 3. House of Thrones.

"They feel it is all made up just to get gullible people to donate money to the churches, to keep the church leaders in clover.

"In fact, the great majority of churches are really nothing at all to do with us as they do not follow the way, and we have our own church, and that is the Son. He is our rock;[10] so do not be taken in with all the talk you hear about the churches, as the Son is our foundation stone and our cornerstone too."

"Okay, thanks Hahuiah; now, can you give me an indication of the role you play in the kingdom of heaven?"

"We do all types of work including the housekeeping and we are all domesticated too. We really enjoy being here together as it is a wonderful place and we enjoy each other's company tremendously.

"And I am the angel who proclaims the news of the day, and I go about informing all of any new disaster that needs looking into, such as an earthquake, or a volcano or tsunami. And I give the people plenty of warning... and the ones who take notice escape, and if the others took notice, they too would escape."

"Do you do anything on a personal level to help the people, Hahuiah?"

"Yes Lee, I am also the one who instructs people on how to get out of trouble in an emergency if they ask, and I need to be there to do that!"

"Can you tell me about some of your personal activities as well?"

"I am always busy and my personal life is intermingled with my work, so I find it hard to tell what is work and what is pleasure as I love all the things I do to help people; and it gives me great satisfaction to see the results of my efforts."

---

[10] In the Bible, (Matthew 16:16) Simon Peter told Jesus that he, Jesus, was the Christ, the Son of the living God. On the strength of Simon's confession of faith, Jesus replied, "...and on this rock I will build my church."

Chapter 3. House of Thrones.

"I would like to add that we are not able to give people help unless they ask for it and also, we cannot force anyone to do anything that is against their wishes. We would love to but it is against Father's rules to do so and this is why so many are not able to get any help when needed. And they are the ones who need help more than any, and we are only able to provide for the faithful.

"We are all able to give comfort to the suffering and we are all able to support those in need; we can also help the others, but usually we wait to be asked and do not give help to them, except if one or more prays, and then we help!"

"Hahuiah, I think a few church-goers will blow a gasket after reading your earlier comments about the majority of churches. But I will leave them in if that's the way it is... and really, who am I to question it? And what did you mean by saying that Christ, the Son is your church?"

"Lee, let it be that the church is the Son and the Son is the church in the minds of the gathered believers, in Christ. And if you feel it will bring trouble to you, omit it; as I have not said this to create any problems, just helping people know about us and what we do!"

"Thanks, Hahuiah, well I guess if that is what the majority of Christians think and believe, I will leave your comments in then."

"Lee, tell them Father enjoys listening to the hymns they sing."

"Okay Hahuiah, and thank you for your time."

God says, "My Son is my church and I have no greater love than the love that I have for Him. Let it be known that all churches in the name of my Son are heading toward me and this is the truth. And I will let all those deemed worthy into my house who worship me and my Son, in my churches."

"Thank you for clarifying that Yahweh."

House of Dominions

Guardian angels residing in this house look after those born
- 23rd July to 2nd September -

God says, "The angels in my House of Dominions do the work of those in the cessation-state and take over their duties in times of great trouble. They help with the work of my angels on duty when they have time to spare and they keep the world running properly as it would stop still without them."

NITHAIAH - looks after those born on 23rd July to 27th July.

"Hello Nithaiah, may I speak to you?"
"Lee, it is Nithaiah!"
"Are you Nithaiah from the House of Dominions?"
"Yes I am and I am the angel in charge here as I have been allocated this role for the rest of the year. The ruling angel has gone on a mission of mercy to keep the world at peace as long as possible until the proper time, as it is written and we are waiting for the awful war to burst into action, killing many, many innocent people.

"The war will escalate and soon the warmongers will be overjoyed as they love to kill each other, especially if they are not on the front line themselves. They enjoy keeping the score and watching it all on television as the football is not as exciting as war and they have a common goal. And they all talk about it in great excitement as they are foolish and they deserve the results that are coming to them. And we will have to sort it all out later and clean up the mess they make of the planet!"

Chapter 4. House of Dominions

"Nithaiah, can you give me some details of your duties and also some information about your private life?"

"Of course, as we all know about the work you are doing and we are trying to be as helpful as possible. And no other book has been written with our personal details in it as we are not prone to telling people about the workings of our houses. You are able to speak to any one of us and also speak to Father, so we trust you implicitly as we know Father would not speak to you otherwise.

"Our Father has given us permission to open our scrolls for you to look at and He has asked us to be as polite as we can be to you. He has asked us to be courteous to you, to provide you with answers to your questions and to be as accurate as possible so you know it to be the truth; and that we are not gilding the lily to make it all sound like a bed of roses, as we have many unpleasant duties to perform, being the watchdogs... and we guard the ones who ask us to."

"Thanks Nithaiah, it's good to know you're helping me with this as it's the first time I've tried interviewing anybody, let alone angels and I'm relying on your co-operation to get the information I need. I've found that even though I'm not asking many questions, most of you have provided me with more than enough to suit my needs as originally these interviews were only going to be about a page long, on each of you."

"Lee, we all have much more to say but we have to keep it brief as we share most of our duties and they overlap each other. It is not hard and fast here but it is whoever is available to do the work at the time and most of us have more than enough to do at any one time. We actually thrive on the pace we work at as it sharpens our wits and keeps us fully occupied; and we need this, as we are all very alert and need maximum activity to provide the sense of accomplishment and job satisfaction that only comes with a job well done."

Chapter 4. House of Dominions

"I can see you differ from most people in that respect then Nithaiah, but then you have no physical body to tire and you don't have to eat or sleep, so you would achieve far more than is possible for a normal living person."

"Lee, I do the work of ten people and it is easy to do and we all do as much and we enjoy it, unlike most people. We want people to do their fair share but this is one of the problems with them as some feel they do not have to work and others feel they should do the work of two. So it is unbalanced and the people suffer unduly because of this, and it should be shared out more evenly so that all have steady employment."

"I agree, Nithaiah, and many unfortunates who cannot gain steady employment or get into business in tough times join the military as a last resort, hoping that they won't get killed in the line of duty and in the hope it will provide an adequate income and a suitable career path. Getting back to that, what are your main duties now that you are in charge of the Dominions?"

"Lee, my duties include instructing the other angels and to delegate the workload, as I read the scrolls. I also keep tabs of what has been done to update the records and keep tabs of the movements of my angels as I want to know where they are at all times. I get them to report to me after each mission and tell me what they have done so that it is written down in the records, exactly as it happens.

"This is why my angels are always truthful as it must be correct or Father will know, and we will be held responsible and accountable for the accuracy of our assessment.

"We know this so all are very careful with it. And we are all keen to make an accurate assessment of the journey as it is the reason why we are here, and we want to do our best."

Chapter 4. House of Dominions

"Thank you for the discussion Nithaiah; hopefully you will have another little chat with me after this task of mine is finished."

"Lee, by all means; feel free to contact me at any time, not after your task is finished but anytime at all, if you want this?"

"Okay; yes, by all means; thanks and goodbye for now."

AHAIAH -   looks after those born on 28th July to 1st August.

"Hello Ahaiah, are you free to speak to me for a minute or two?"
"Lee, it is Ahaiah!"
"Are you Ahaiah from the House of Dominions?"
"Lee, it is me, Ahaiah, an angel from the House of Dominions."
"Ahaiah, can you provide me with a few details about your duties and also give me a few details about your personal life?"

"It will be my pleasure to give you the information you seek. I am the angel who lets people have the freedom they enjoy so much. And I tell them to strive for a democratic society and not accept less than that... and that is why slavery is not allowed anymore. I have been watching over the nations to keep my eye on this as some unscrupulous people are still using slaves in many ways.

"I am the one who is to stop this by letting others know. And I keep my eyes open and keep myself aware of the people who are in this - and they are in my bad books. I have their names written down so that when the Day of Judgment is upon them they will be cast out and they will suffer dreadfully for their deeds!"

"Yes I know, Ahaiah, a lot of countries turn a blind eye to slavery and many people are kept under these conditions to create wealth for unscrupulous, unethical and greedy business people."

Chapter 4. House of Dominions

"Lee, the world is full of wickedness and people will do anything if they feel they can get away with it; but they forget or do not know that they will pay for their sins. And it is divine in this way as they are to be punished justly... and they are to be shown for what they are, to all!

"Let it be seen that future generations will be rewarded in the way they will not allow these people access to industry and they will be tabbed as unsuitable employers by special departments set up to scrutinize them.

"As civilization progresses and the influences of evil are extinguished, life for all will be worth living as checks and balances will be put in place to ascertain that all disadvantaged people have access to the basic necessities without having to compromise themselves or their families."

"Can you give me a few details about yourself now, Ahaiah?"

"I am the angel who loves visiting little children and whenever I can, I visit them and play games with them to keep them happy. I give them joy by being their invisible friend and they talk to me and confide in me. And I hear their little voices telling me their secrets and their joys and their hurts and my heart overflows with love for them.

"This is my pastime and I have the privilege of being able to do this - and my heart is gladdened whenever I am with them. I want this to go on for as long as is possible until they grow up and cannot see or hear me anymore; but plenty of children see me and hear me and I am here for them."

"That's interesting Ahaiah, as I've heard of children having invisible friends, and now I know it's possibly you or one of the other angels. Thank you very much for doing this for them, I'll look forward to speaking to you again shortly; goodbye for now."

"Lee, the pleasure is all mine as I know that you are doing a lot of good among the people, and you will be helping us later on as will the messenger Golaiah. I will bid you farewell for now and God bless you."

Chapter 4. House of Dominions

YERATEL - looks after those born on 2nd August to 6th August.

"Hello Yeratel, are you able to speak to me for a few minutes?"
"Lee, it is Yeratel!"
"Are you Yeratel, an angel from the House of Dominions?"
"Yes, I am he and I am the angel in the Dominions who looks after the people in homes for the aged and geriatric centers.

"I look after these people to ensure they are happy. And if not I bring it to the attention of those who can do something about it, as I want the elderly to be just as happy as they were when they were young.

"It is nice to be watching over them as they chat to each other bringing up stories about their lives, reminiscing about them; and this lets them cope as they can release the feelings that they have pent up inside.

"They are slowly diminishing in intellect so it is a natural transition to cross-over this way and it is far easier to adjust this way; and it is a happy change for them and a glad day for them.

"It is a wonderful time for them when they are reunited once more with their loved ones who died before they did; and they rejoice as they are together again once more to share their times and tales.

"And they weep with joy and are overcome with emotion at having their friends and loved ones with them once more, as the loneliness of old age is apparent when they remember those who have gone before them. They have lived to see all those go before them; and I weep too sometimes at seeing how happy they are, and I share in their joy too!"

"Well, you certainly carry out admirable duties Yeratel, thank you for letting me know. Now, what else would you like you tell me about yourself that may be of interest to the people?"

"Lee, I exist only for others and my joy comes from helping others. When people realize how important it is to be good to those with whom

Chapter 4. House of Dominions

they share their lives, then they are well on the way to becoming higher beings spiritually. And the way the world is heading they need to hurry as it will be too late for most.

"And they will wish they had spent more time helping others, rather than helping themselves... and this is a big lesson for them to learn."

"Thank you for your insights and comments Yeratel; goodbye for now and keep up the good work!"

"I am always here Lee, and if you need any more information let me know and I will provide it for you!"

"Okay, thanks Yeratel, I'll speak to you again soon; goodbye."

SEHAIAH - looks after those born on 7th August to 12th August.

"Hello Sehaiah, are you free for a few minutes?"
"Lee, it is Sehaiah!"
"Are you Sehaiah from the House of Dominions?"
"Yes Lee, it is! I am the one you seek."

"Sehaiah, I would like to know if you can give me some sort of insight into the duties you carry out in your daily routine and also what you do in your spare time."

"Lee, I do many different things and sometimes, during the course of the day I will intervene in the lives of people who run the risk of losing their life. I stop them somehow from doing anything foolish that puts their life in jeopardy.

"And I keep them from doing anymore stupid things, as I want them to remain alive to carry out the role they are destined for. If it seems to be their destiny to die, I let them die and if it doesn't seem to be their destiny, I stop them and keep them from killing themselves."

Chapter 4. House of Dominions

"Then the world will remain on course for the future in store for it without another hiccup as all have a small part to play - and all things seem meant to be. And all things seem to be for a reason even though they may not be apparent to us immediately, as we all have free will to do whatever we please.

"Nevertheless, the general overall destiny is predetermined as Father can see the future as no other can, and Father knows the role each individual has. And He makes it happen if He wants to but usually He does not interfere with the running of people's lives."

"Thank you Sehaiah, now can you give me a few details about your personal life or anything else you may wish to add?"

"Yes Lee, I would like to say a few things to the readers of this book. I would emphasize to all of you who are able to do so, to go and see if you can do something about the children who are going without in your neighborhood as the problems are constantly escalating, while greed and corruption overtake sanity! The politicians are only glorifying their own names, not knowing want nor hunger and never having been without; not knowing the problems faced by those without any money and without any hope of making any money.

"The wealthy look down on those without and snicker and scoff and say to each other, 'It is their own fault that they are poor and living in poverty; it is entirely their own fault that they have nothing.' But it is circumstance alone and the educated will be asked why they did not help them; and they will say that they did not realize what was happening before their very own eyes. Then we will snicker and scoff at their story of ignorance, and we will say to them that they are to be educated in the manner Father has decided for them!"

"Do you have any personal comments you would like to say about yourself now, Sehaiah?"

Chapter 4. House of Dominions

"Lee, I am going to be there on the Day of Judgment, overseeing the people who are being transported between the different realms and all I can say is that if they are not listening to this, then they will deserve to suffer the consequences, as we are telling them! And if they do not listen, then they will be very sorry!"

"Thanks Sehaiah, goodbye for now."

"Lee, it is my pleasure and I will give you any information you need."

"Thanks for the offer Sehaiah and if I get the chance, I'll come back for more; goodbye."

REIYEL - looks after those born on 13th August to 17th August.

"Hello Reiyel, may I speak to you for a few minutes?"

"Lee, it is Reiyel!"

"Are you Reiyel, an angel from the House of Dominions?"

"Yes Lee, I am the angel who looks after the people who are in danger when traveling either by bus, train, boat or plane. I save many lives daily by diverting disasters from the people I look after and I have the ability to be everywhere at once as we all do here. We have the ability to see all and hear all as we angels are omnipresent, having many more senses than mortal man."

"Reiyel, you mean to say you can be anywhere you want to be or everywhere at the same time?"

"Yes, we angels have this ability, as while you are at your desk at any one moment in time, at the same moment our thoughts are everywhere. We are able to travel much faster and communicate our thoughts much more quickly than humankind could comprehend, as we have different times and distances from what you have; and we have many different senses, unknown to you. We are many times more powerful than you

Chapter 4. House of Dominions

think and are very quick in our work; and we can be doing more than one task at a time, if we wish."

"Reiyel, have you ever saved the life of any one individual more than once; and if so, how many times?"

"Yes I have, Lee. During the Napoleonic Wars a soldier prayed daily and I saved his life from cannon fire, the sword and falling from his steed many times; and he beseeched his fellow soldiers to pray likewise. But they scoffed and most died slowly from horrific wounds and suffered tremendously. This particular soldier was saved from death at least five times, as I remember!"

"What sort of man was Napoleon, Reiyel?"

"He was intolerably cruel and had a sadistic streak, enjoying death; and he mostly enjoyed watching soldiers die in agony, as this gave him immense pleasure and was the driving force behind his many wars. He was a madman as all who enjoy war are."

"What sort of punishment will Napoleon get when the Day of Judgment is upon him, Reiyel?"

"His fate is sealed and he will perish after he has reviewed his crimes against humanity and has felt the pain and suffering he created. So his future is bleak and he awaits this with great trepidation. And now he weeps as he knows of his pending fate and does not want to go through the agonies he suffered others to go through.

"His soul is still on the earth plane waiting for the time to arrive when Father will summon him before all of us, for him to account for his crimes and for him to be told of the dreadful consequences he is going to suffer, and of the severity of the punishment he will receive."

"Would you like to tell me about your personal life now, Reiyel?"

"Lee, I love artwork and I watch the people make their artwork and I watch the buildings being constructed; but mostly I love the temples in

Chapter 4. House of Dominions

the Middle East, and the ancient buildings in Rome and in Greece too; as I love the architecture, originally impressing my own ideas into the minds of and inspiring the designers of these buildings of yesteryear."

"Thanks Reiyel, would you like to say anything else?"

"Yes Lee, during the time of King Herod the Great, I was watching over the baby Jesus and helped Mary and Joseph escape into the land of Egypt. Herod was a very cruel man and he put all the children up to the age of two to death in his land, and this caused much anguish; and he hurt his people to the point of rebellion."

"I've heard about that awful saga Reiyel, and Herod, another madman, will also have to face the consequences of his dreadful actions shortly."

"Yes Lee, the world is in turmoil at the moment and the results will be evident soon. So those in charge of the nations had better take heed as the time of judgment is at hand, and they have much to make amends for. The prophecies are being fulfilled and the world is ruled by the wicked. And the wicked will pay for the way they are leading the people into war. These wicked rulers have no conscience about the lies they tell and no compassion for the people seeking refuge; and no compassion for the women with little ones who are being killed every day by the destructive weapons of war they have. And soon they must answer for this - as the writing is on the wall!

"They will suffer more than is imaginable for their crimes against humanity; and if they were to beg to be forgiven they would be, but will still have to suffer the punishment due, to put it right in the minds of those watching. And to make amends would be impossible... so they will perish. My Father is going to discipline them first and He will vent His wrath on them; and they will wish they had not ever been born."

"Reiyel, thank you for the time you've spent with me today, which you did obligingly, though I sense you are needed elsewhere."

Chapter 4. House of Dominions

"Yes Lee, but it was worthwhile as we have spoken about many other things in private during our time together. We have begun a friendship here today that will be everlasting and I know this; and your role is to be part of the upcoming events which are to unfold shortly."

"Okay, thank you Reiyel; goodbye for now."

OMAEL - looks after those born on 18th August to 22nd August.

"Hello Omael, are you free to speak to me for a minute or two?"

"Lee, it is Omael, an angel from the House of Dominions and my role is to give the others and the people my drive and ambition as I have plenty. The reason I do this is to keep the people motivated and not allow them to become slovenly, and not to become lazy like the others."

"The others? Do you mean the other angels, Omael?"

"Yes, as some of the younger ones are prone to playing games and to forgetting their heavenly roles. They are prone to gallivanting about enjoying themselves, playing Cupid and playing the matchmaker; having a wonderful time instead of putting their noses to the grindstone, doing the work that I tell them to do."

"So, do you lead by example, Omael?"

"We all do and we set an example to the younger angels as we are here to do our God given duties, not our own work which is not in the script, but the work of our Father which means looking after the people and their needs.

"I keep the people interested in their work by rewarding them with the purchases they make, and they are kept motivated by buying their cars and paying them off, and some are buying houses too. The people need to be reminded that if they do not pay off their purchases the economy will grind to a halt. That is why the government is always taxing them, to

Chapter 4. House of Dominions

make certain that the roads are made and that they, the people, will have a higher standard of living if they make a contribution. Those who do not are not able to help with the national growth as they are idle and do not earn money, and they do not reap the benefits that come from working.

"And the ones who work the hardest are paid less as they are my friends and are not blinded by greed, and they are always willing to help others. And the ones who work little and paid more are not my friends, as they are usually the ones who do nothing to help others."

"Thanks Omael, is there anything else you would like to add to that; perhaps something personal about yourself?"

"Lee, my personal life is not actually personal as all here can hear and can see what I do, though I must say that I really enjoy listening to the songs that are played on the radio. And I am enraptured with the music as it is very pleasant, and it is very different from the harps and the flutes and the trumpets and the other instruments that we have here; and I find it enthralling, and find it delightful to the ear."

"Well I'm pleased to hear that you enjoy the songs and the music so much Omael, thank you for your contribution; goodbye for now."

"Lee, thank you for your time also as you have spent many hours speaking to us and to our Father; you have gained much more knowledge about us and that is good. You can impart this to the people and some will probably want to know more! Goodbye Lee and God bless you!"

"Okay, thanks Omael; goodbye."

Chapter 4. House of Dominions

LECABEL - looks after those born on 23rd August to 28th August.

"Hello Lecabel, do you have time to stop work and speak to me for a little while?"

"Lee, it is Lecabel!"

"Are you Lecabel an angel from the House of Dominions?"

"I am Lecabel, the same and I am able to speak to you for as long as you like as you have asked our Father to supply me with helpers. The helpers are here today doing my work with me and they are glad to help, and I am glad too."

"That's very good to hear, Lecabel. Now, can you tell me what you do in the house and a little about yourself, if possible?"

"Lee, my duties are to keep my eye on the house and I am always at home, not being one to leave the house often, as I have a quiet personality. I would rather be in my own little abode than be in the cathedral or visiting others. I enjoy studying my scrolls and I enjoy reading and I read many things in all languages as we can converse in any language here.

"We all have that ability, to translate our thoughts into the language of the recipient no matter what that language may be. I listen to people speaking Chinese and understand them and I listen to people speaking English, Spanish and Russian and understand them all too. All is by and large, the same, as speech is to convey messages and ideas; and we are truly messengers though we are guardians first and foremost."

"Well, that's interesting Lecabel, would you like to say anything else?"

"Lee, I would, but it is not my style to talk about myself as I am not an extrovert. I am reserved in my speech; so just say that I can do the work of any other if someone else wants to go somewhere, and I help out in the house whenever I find something that needs to be done."

Chapter 4. House of Dominions

"I keep the other angels' scrolls in order and look after their personal needs by reminding them when they have an appointment. And I remind them of the people seeking help from them, especially if they have overlooked anyone, for the reason of being too busy.

"I also remind them when they are to go to the house of another to learn or to teach, whatever the case may be; and I keep myself occupied with these things, very much like a busy housekeeper or administrator; and this keeps our house running efficiently."

"Okay, Lecabel; thank you for your time and your contribution."

"Goodbye Lee, will I see you again shortly?"

"Yes Lecabel, remind me if I forget. Thank you; goodbye for now."

VASAIAH - looks after those born on 29th August to 2nd September.

"Hello Vasaiah, may I speak to you about your duties for a few minutes?"

"Lee?"

"Yes, Vasaiah, are you an angel from the House of Dominions?"

"I am and my duties are my personal business! I am reluctant to tell you of them as you have no right to ask and I have no inclination to tell you!"

"That's entirely up to you Vasaiah. The only reason I'm asking you is to let people know what you do in the heavenly realms, how much work you do for them and how much help you provide them with."

"Then tell them that I do much more for them than they do for me! I have been working my backside off for thousands of years looking after them and not many ever thank us or even acknowledge us! And even more who do know of us slander us and tell each other we are not here

Chapter 4. House of Dominions

for them any longer, either to suit the doctrine of their church or to suit some other silly whim that has overtaken their tiny minds!

"And I am telling you straight... I am fed up with all of you! And you can all go and get future help from the other angels, as I am not going to help anymore! I have told Father and He has told me to take it easy as there are now other helpers you have asked Him to provide! I am the one who deserves a rest now as I have worked tirelessly for many years! And for what?"

"Vasaiah, our Father will provide you with rewards for all of your labors and then you will see that it was all worthwhile. Take things quietly for now and relax awhile until you calm down and feel better, as the Day of Judgment will be upon us all shortly and your work will be finished. Then you can take it easy, reaping the rewards Father has made ready for you."

"Thank you for reminding me and I am sorry for being so peevish. I am usually very congenial and rarely say a word in anger, but today is different as I see all the unnecessary killing that is going on in Afghanistan! And I really am wondering if it is worth all the trouble looking after the human race anymore! We all suffer the consequences when war breaks out between nations!

"And this is supposedly a fight against terrorism, though the millions of displaced people bearing the brunt of it have little or no idea of what is going on as they are poor and defenseless, with little food or water!

"Many are now dying in freezing conditions in mud huts or tents, or in the open desert without any amenities! What do you think of it all, Lee?"

"Vasaiah, the proper way to fight terrorism is to capture the actual perpetrators and bring them to justice instead of bombing Afghanistan back into the stone-age, destroying their towns and villages. We are told the people there will find new found democratic freedoms later on but it

Chapter 4. House of Dominions

would appear from cynical anti-war media reports from Europe that the real long-term agenda is to implement a change of leadership there, control the oil and gas pipelines and gradually siphon up to six trillion dollars worth of mineral resources from out of there and other neighboring regions of the Middle East, such as Iraq."

"Yes, all that will eventually happen, Lee, but the people are mainly worried about their own safety at the moment and millions are fleeing the country through the desert. And they are drowning in the sea as the fishing boats are unsafe to travel in, and they have nowhere safe to go.

"This makes me both sad and angry and if I had my own way I would stop it. But it is part of the prophecies and a sign that the end is nigh, so I just sit here shaking my head at it all and wonder why God our Father lets them do this!"

"We all have free will, Vasaiah, and many things that are evil are perpetrated daily against all common decency, but in the end all wrong doers will be punished according to God's rules and wishes."

"Lee, you are right and I am not thinking about later, but this moment, as this injustice is happening right now and it is in front of us right now. I cringe when I see this and I feel passionately that we should be stopping it but it has to be, as humankind is perpetrating it and this is what they want to do. And we are supposed to help them whenever they pray to Father, but they are doing wrong!

"The only solace we have is that they will all have to look at the results when they are eventually called to account for their misdeeds. All are made to take responsibility for their actions and all are made to pay the price for these actions! And all will regret their actions!"

"Well, Thanks Vasaiah, you have made a significant contribution after all and I will keep in touch; goodbye for now."

"Goodbye, Lee, and thank you, I will contact you again soon."

House of Virtues

Guardian angels residing in this house look after those born
- 3rd September to 13th October -

God says, "The angels in my House of Virtues are my miracle workers and I send them to intervene in situations that I personally want changed. They do this for me as they are the ones who perform miracles on earth!"

<u>**YEHUIAH**</u> - looks after those born on 3rd September to 7th September.

"Hello Yehuiah, have you any time free to speak to me?"
"Lee, it is Yehuiah; you may speak to me for as long as you please."
"Thank you; are you an angel from the House of Virtues?"
"Yes I am and I look after the people who need help in matters that are of a sensitive nature, and I look after the intimate details and tell them the right way to go about getting their wishes met.

"I give them hope when all seems lost as I tell them how to go about making their dreams come true. I give them hope when they feel that all is against them and I look right into the heart of matters for them, which enables me to come up with a solution - and they are usually surprised at the results and are sometimes left in a state of disbelief!"

"It would be good to have you on our team batting for us then, Yehuiah. Most people would love to have you helping them make their dreams come true."

"Lee, the people who ask for help are usually in a tight spot and pray to Father to give them solutions to their immediate problems, so He sends me to sort it out for them. I do the best I can and sometimes I do

Chapter 5. House of Virtues.

more than I realize as they are often overjoyed at what seems to be a very natural answer, but to them it seems as though it is a miracle come true!"

"It must give you a deep sense of satisfaction to be able to get such a positive response to your work Yehuiah, and you probably get quite a lot of requests for help too."

"Yes, you are correct and my workload is never ending which to me is a blessing as I do not like being idle, so I put everything into my work, and I love my work."

"Is there anything else you would like to share with us, Yehuiah?"

"I have likes and dislikes as we all do and I love to watch the people walking along the streets going from one place to another. And I find it interesting to see them, a never-ending stream of people coming and going and I often wonder why they need to walk from here to there.

"My pastime is to find out how far some people travel in one day on foot and out of curiosity I watch how far some people walk, as it seems that they may be walking for important reasons, going on appointments or simply exercising."

"Are these people you follow around as your pastime, the same people you are assigned to watch over as part of your main duties as a guardian angel, Yehuiah?"

"Yes Lee, usually they are and I watch them to ensure they are safe and I watch them to keep them heading in the right direction and I watch out for them in other ways too."

"Is there anything else you do that may be of interest to our readers, Yehuiah?"

"I cannot vouch for that Lee, but I go to sporting events and sometimes if a team needs my help and they have prayed to Father, I gently give them the leading edge. And if my intuition tells me that it will

Chapter 5. House of Virtues.

bring great joy to my flock to see this team win, I give this team the victory by instilling my ideas into their minds, to run with."

"Thank you Yehuiah, it has been interesting speaking to you and I'll let you get on with your duties, goodbye for now."

"Goodbye Lee, thank you for asking me to speak to you."

LEHAHIAH - looks after those born on 8th September to 12th September.

"Hello Lehahiah, are you available for an interview right now?"

"Lee, it is Lehahiah!"

"Are you Lehahiah, an angel from the House of Virtues?"

"I am, and I believe you want to ask me about my duties and to ask me to give you a brief account of my personal life?"

"Yes Lehahiah, I do and it's to let the people reading this have an idea of what guardian angels do, apart from saving their lives when they're in danger, as some people probably think you're constantly walking alongside them all day, the same way a bodyguard does."

"Lee, that is not correct and we do not stay with any one person for long, only long enough to help when they require it and then we move on to the next mission. My duties include encouraging certain selected people to reach great heights in their chosen field. And I give them my personal best as I believe that to encourage a gifted individual is a very worthy cause, as sadly, most gifted people are wasted and do not reach anywhere near their full potential."

"I see, so you help some people create works of art, design products or invent things, is that the sort of thing you do?"

"Exactly, and we give them detailed instructions on how to achieve this and they think it is inspirational, but in reality it is us implanting the thoughts into their minds - and if they listen to their intuition carefully,

Chapter 5. House of Virtues.

they will be able to produce remarkable results as most new inventions are created in this way."

"Lehahiah, I believe that inventive people like Nikola Tesla received ideas in this way as he invented many remarkable products, including alternating electrical current (AC) and the Tesla coil."

"Correct Lee, and we do this to help people along in their careers as well as to advance the human race, which has been more than obvious during the last century, and this will continue."

"What else would you like to tell me about, Lehahiah?"

"Lee, the people are getting more and more restless, and they are getting the idea that something out of the ordinary is going to happen shortly and they are right. There are going to be some changes on the planet earth soon and people will have to adjust to this and this will create a lot of problems for some, but most will cope and this is going to become evident within five years from now.

"It will bring a lot of destruction to the planet so be warned now. And be conscious of the effects that polluting the atmosphere will have, and be aware of what is happening to the planet you live on. Try to become more environmentally aware and also start conserving energy and other resources."

"Okay, I will try my very best to learn more and do more for the environment; thanks, Lehahiah. Now, would you like to discuss your hobbies?"

"Yes Lee, thank you for the time you have given us all and this is my pleasure to spend time with you and the others as my time is well spent in good company. And this is good company... and this is my hobby to be in good company; goodbye and thank you."

"Thank you for your good company too, Lehahiah, it has been a very interesting conversation; goodbye."

Chapter 5. House of Virtues.

CHAVAKIAH - looks after those born on 13th September to 17th September.

"Hello Chavakiah, have you got a few minutes free to let me know about your role and what you do in the House of Virtues?"

"Hello Lee! Yes by all means!"

"Are you Chavakiah, an angel from the House of Virtues?"

"I am, and thank you for asking me to speak to you, to make a contribution to your book about us. I am overjoyed at the prospect of seeing my words in print and having my words published. I feel it is about time people knew about us as we have been long forgotten by most people, and I want to say a few things too."

"Feel free to say whatever you like, Chavakiah as we would like to know about the responsibilities you have in heaven and on earth, and about anything else you do here and there in your own free time."

"Lee, I work in counseling and my time is spent speaking to the lost souls who arrive in the light from the earth plane after many years of torment and anguish, as they have refused to come here for their own particular reasons. I talk to them about these reasons and purge them of their hurt and I counsel them to begin anew without all the hang-ups and without bringing those issues into the light with them, as they need to forget all this and move on, to a better future.

"They are supposed to learn from the past, not remain in it suffering from long past grievances. And this is my main duty, to look after these poor lost souls just arriving after deciding to let go and come to the light, which is in the here and now, not leaving them to remain locked in the past, but to begin life again with a fresh outlook with new friends, new ideas and new adventures to look forward to."

"That sounds like very interesting work Chavakiah, what do you do to

Chapter 5. House of Virtues.

relax and unwind between such heavy counseling sessions?"

"Lee, I never really relax as that is my natural state of being anyway, and to ask me that is like asking, are you lax? And that is not me as I enjoy the position I hold here as Chief Counselor of Lost Souls. I enjoy talking to lost souls all day, telling them how to become more than they ever knew they could be.

"And the joy it gives me is beyond words as it is an emotional bonding between me, the lost souls, God and the universe as they become aware of all that is. And they are enlightened up to the point they are entitled to be, and this is uplifting for me. So you see, it is not my style to relax on the job"

"Chavakiah, I meant after your duties are finished and you have free time, what do you do with any spare time you have left?"

"This is the time I spend by myself reflecting on my attitude, trying to better understand others. Sometimes my ego is in overdrive and I put my foot in my mouth as you have just seen. So I do have to reflect on my own behavior sometimes as we all do. From this... from this we grow and become better in ourselves as we strive to become the enlightened beings we hope to be, and be able to be seen in the proper light as kind and loving individuals.

"We are trying to attain the highest level of enlightenment possible and we are all striving toward that. You are an inspiration to us as you have already attained level seven, being an old soul and having more experience in life than nearly all here and we ask you to guide us and give us of your knowledge too."

"By all means Chavakiah, and if I can be of assistance to you, please let me know. Goodbye for now and we will catch up again soon."

"Lee, please come back and help me with some of my difficult cases soon! Goodbye!"

Chapter 5. House of Virtues.

MENADEL -   looks after those born on 18th September to 23rd September.

"Hello Menadel, do you have a few minutes free to speak to me?"
"Hello Lee, it is Menadel!"
"Are you Menadel, an angel from the House of Virtues?"
"Yes, it is Menadel from the House of Virtues. And what is it you would like to know?"
"Menadel, I'm letting the people who read this know a little about guardian angels by individually asking each one of you to give me an insight into your personal daily activities, and any other interesting information about yourself that you would like to divulge."
"Lee, my duties are to bring deceased souls from the earth plane to the realms they belong to."
"Are these lost souls Menadel, or souls of the recently deceased?"
"Lee, the souls are from the earth plane and they are either freshly released or long forgotten souls. And I bring them here to have them scrutinized and questioned as to their religious beliefs and their long held views. We see if any of their beliefs are true or not and then we decide whether to re-educate them or leave them alone, depending on the beliefs they have. All are entitled to find the truth... and they are eventually taught this truth and will be judged on this later.

"I also bring the latest news to the other angels in our house and I give them my version of it. I edit a lot of it as a lot is superfluous and would clutter their busy lives. Another duty I have is to bring forgiven souls here to our house to be cleansed. I feel that the duties I perform are very valuable as some people who are praying to Father ask for the souls of those they love to be cleansed and freed from sin, and this is what I do."

Chapter 5. House of Virtues.

"Can you elaborate on that Menadel, the bit about asking Father to cleanse the souls?"

"Yes Lee, the dead are to be judged on their beliefs and that is also part of the Judgment as all are to be judged on the way they have conducted themselves during life.

"All are initially judged by the Order of Angels at the time of death, to find their level of spiritual awareness. A great many spirits get promoted from a lower level to a higher level in the light, having been forgiven of their sins either by being prayed for or by having spent enough time on the level that Father had deemed necessary for them.

"In any case I help them by not only escorting them to the higher level attained but also by bringing their records up to date; taking them to the House of Cherubim, locating their personal records and updating them."

"Is there some sort of ceremony to this cleansing, Menadel?"

"Lee, the cathedrals are for any services we hold and yes, this service is held for them in the House of Virtues at a specified time as there are always plenty of new arrivals and our large cathedral has many souls attending the service for, 'The Ceremony of Cleansed Souls.'"

"Well, that's something to know Menadel; I've heard about the cathedrals in the light before from another angel but had little idea as to what went on in them, apart from their being reserved for the judgment."

"Lee, we do not stand on ceremony here and attendance is voluntary. The hymns are beautiful to listen to and if you are in the vicinity, you will find the singing is absolutely divine as they practice day after day to occupy their time. It has reached a remarkable degree, the pinnacle of excellence, and it is truly magnificent to see and most uplifting to hear!"

"What do you do when you get some free time, Menadel?"

"I play one of the instruments in the orchestra in my spare time, and this is my life."

Chapter 5. House of Virtues.

"Thanks for all your interesting comments Menadel, and for giving me this information. It's wonderful to hear that so much activity is going on in heaven; goodbye for now."

"Goodbye Lee, it has been a pleasure to speak to you again."

HANIEL - looks after those born on 24th September to 28th September.

"Hello Haniel, it is Lee here!"

"Lee? Are you here to interview me?"

"Yes, are you Haniel, an angel from the House of Virtues?"

"Lee, yes I am; pleased to meet you!"

"Thank you Haniel, I'm pleased to meet you too. Would you mind giving me some details about the work you do in your house and some details about your private life too, if that's possible?"

"Lee, it will be a pleasure to tell you about my life here as no-one has ever asked me before. All who contact us want help and no-one has ever offered any. So it is remarkable that for the first time in history someone has come here and offered help to us in some way."

"Oh! Okay, now I understand what you mean Haniel. You mean the help you got by my asking Yahweh to supply more helpers for all of you and attending to some of the other more private matters that He sorted out for you?"

"Yes, we are all very grateful and we are very pleased now and most of us, that is, about ninety-nine percent of us have been really pleased with the things you have asked Father to do for us... and our lives have changed for the better.

"We were surprised to say the least as all others have taken from us and no-one has given. So you are the first to do this, and we are very, very pleased."

Chapter 5. House of Virtues.

"Thank you Haniel, I'm pleased too. It's good to know that my efforts are appreciated."

"Lee, we appreciate what you have done for us and now you are typing this information down to show the people about us. This too will help us as people will know our names and know what we do and become familiar with our domains. And they will ask us to help them without fear, knowing we are here and we can be here for them.

"You can help too if they need to know any more about us, and you are supplying Father's personal scroll to the people shortly - and they will read this and will understand more.

"The people will be fascinated and they will inundate you with many questions that only they could dream up. And they will ask you about the beginning and about the end and ask you all sorts of questions as they will all want to know the answers.

"You will have to evade them and tell them to read the book you are going to publish with the words of our Father in, and this will keep them happy."

"I hope to keep them happy Haniel, as 'The Word' as Yahweh wants his last word and testament called, is being written for everyone to read, though there will be a few surprises in store for many people, including many people who think they are good Christians, as well."

"Lee, I am taking up far too much of your time so I will tell you about myself now. I update the records here and I do the scheduling of events as well as arrange the timetables to suit each house.

"I synchronize the events so that they all run like clockwork and arrange the concerts that are held regularly in the cathedrals; and I schedule meetings among the elders and look after the younger angels, showing them the ropes."

Chapter 5. House of Virtues.

"I do standby work too if someone is too overloaded to attend to an emergency so my life is really a whirlwind of activity, and I love it and I could not think of a better team to work with or a better place to be."

"Haniel, can you tell me a little about your personal activities now?"

"Lee, yes of course. I do a lot of things such as visit the sick and dying and help those out in dire straits. And I try to get the people who pray to Father out of the many predicaments they find themselves in.

"I stop the wind if a sailboat is capsizing, I stop the fire if there is a child in a burning house; I stop the car if it is going to crash, and I stop the bullet from killing if the man or woman is asking God to save them; and I tell others to 'phone for help if someone is in trouble.

"I do many things to save the people who ask for help and even if they have not got time to ask, I help out if I can. And sometimes I do it just to save them and sometimes I do it to deliberately stop them from being harmed by a demon.

"Sometimes I stop the judge from handing out the death penalty if that person is innocent or has been framed and I always try to see that my flock is justly tried and treated with respect."

"Haniel, you are certainly kept busy. Thank you for your help and I'll keep in touch with you; goodbye for now and keep up the good work."

"Lee, it is a pleasure and I will give you much more information if you need it... and if you do not need it I will just tell you about the incidents that happen, so that you are informed of what is going on around you; goodbye my friend."

"Okay then, thanks Haniel; very much appreciated, goodbye."

Chapter 5. House of Virtues.

HAAMIAH -   looks after those born on 29th September to 3rd October.

"Hello Haamiah, have you got time to speak to me for a few minutes?"
"Hello Lee, yes I am free."
"Are you Haamiah, an angel from the House of Virtues?"
"Yes Lee, and I am going to give you a story about the way we work and rotate our work to suit. We all pitch in as we do at times to help each other. And we have a wonderful camaraderie here as we are all united. We enjoy many times when we are together and join in with meetings and debate on things that need fixing on earth.

"And we try to solve the problems by pricking the consciences of humans, trying to make them change their minds. We are successful most of the time, but the times we are not are the times that we are needed the most, and you are in the final days now.

"The world leaders are corrupt and have no compassion. They are Satan's emissaries and have no idea of common decency as they are blinded by his ways. And the people who listen to them are just as bad and will be forsaken as well."

"Well, thanks for that, Haamiah. It does seem that we're in the last days as you say, and the world is certainly becoming a hostile place to be in and seems to be getting worse all the time. What do you do when you take a break away from all this disgraceful behavior?"

"Lee, we have many helpers now and we have you to thank for that. Whenever I have free time, I go away to contemplate the future and pray that I will be one of the angels to sit with Father in conference when the time of judgment is here upon us, as I will tell all.

"I am keeping records for this day as I am horrified at all the wicked people who are on earth and I must make certain they are thrown into the pit to perish. And good riddance to bad rubbish, I say!"

Chapter 5. House of Virtues.

"I think that bottomless pit will be very full after the day of reckoning, Haamiah, as there are people not only from this day and age but from throughout history who have to be judged as well and it will be far, far better for everyone remaining here to be without them at all."

"Lee, we will be safe from the evil they produce and all will be well, for then the people left will be kind to each other and share their food and take good care of each other."

"I'll say goodbye now, Haamiah. Yahweh has just told me to tell you He has approved of your request to be one of those sitting in with Him on Judgment Day. Goodbye and good luck for now."

"Goodbye Lee, this is the best news I have ever had, thank you!"

REHAEL - looks after those born on 4th October to 8th October.

"Hello Rehael, I would like to speak to you if you have some free time to spare."

"Yes Lee, it is Rehael. Firstly, I had better let you know how to pronounce my name as you seem to have no idea and secondly, I want the readers to know how I like my name pronounced as well!"

"Alright Rehael; are you Rehael, an angel from the House of Virtues?"

"I am the Rehael from this house and my name is pronounced as Ryell, not sounding the 'aitch.' I am surprised none of the others have mentioned how you mispronounce their names. Their names are from the time when I was an angel overseeing the land of Israel. The angels speak in the original language we used then and that was in Old Hebrew."

"Oh! Rehael, I used to make a point of getting the angels to pronounce their names for me and I have written a fair few of them down too as they are hard for me to remember. Only angels like you that I haven't

Chapter 5. House of Virtues.

contacted before are the ones who haven't got the proper pronunciations written down in my little reference book. What did you say the main language you use now is?"

"Lee, we speak in Old Hebrew at home in our own environment and although we speak all languages as we have been able to from the beginning of time, we write our scrolls in this Hebrew and we converse to each other in Hebrew. This is our native language and we regard other languages as a way of differentiating the people and this is one of the ways we know who they are.

"And we tried to keep the people separate as it was not the way we thought, that they should change from one place to another, except for this day as it is now shown to us by our Father that this is to happen.

"And this is a sign that the world has become saturated with too many souls to keep and they have to travel from one place to the next seeking refuge in other lands to find a better life. I watch this and we are wondering if Father knew that this would happen as we had no idea.

"And Father does not let us have knowledge at our meetings as to His future plans as he feels we have enough to contend with from day to day, let alone worry about the future too."

"Rehael, I have noticed that every time an angel speaks to me they nearly always start off with my name so that no-one in the spirit world is left in any doubt as to who is being addressed.

"Also, you all tend to say as much as possible at once without breaking your speech into a two way conversation, relentlessly continuing on with one sentence after another, usually starting and joining each clause with the conjunction 'and' without a break in between."

"Lee, the reason for this is that Father speaks to us in this manner and it gives us a considerable amount of information without having to ask

Chapter 5. House of Virtues.

more questions. And it conveys and explains exactly what needs to be said in one. This is our way of speaking to each other, having spoken this way for many thousands of years and when translated into your language it is expressed poorly, but in our language it is the best way for us to convey a message. Let it be remembered that language changes constantly and this language you have now is derived from many.

"We have learned to listen to it all, and we listen to many different languages all day. We can also communicate with you, letting you have our knowledge and we impart this knowledge to you through your mind and through your ears too, if you try to hear us!

"I must bid you farewell right now Lee, as I am needed elsewhere; goodbye."

"Okay, thank you very much for being here Rehael, it's very much appreciated; goodbye."

IEIAZEL -   looks after those born on 9th October to 13th October.

"Hello Ieiazel, are you there?"

"Lee, I am free so if you want to interview me, now is a good time for it!"

"Okay, thanks Ieiazel, are you an angel from the House of Virtues?"

"Yes Lee, I am your personal guardian angel and ever since you were born I have always been nearby to see you were being looked after. I have helped you numerous times in your youth, letting you have a few things that would not normally have been obtainable to you then and I have watched over you for many years, keeping you under my wing.

"I have been looking after you in other matters too, providing you with three spirit guides and they are all doing your bidding if only you knew it. They look after you daily, as I have not been here to do this all the time,

Chapter 5. House of Virtues.

having many, many other people to watch over. This keeps me just about fully occupied as well as carrying out my other duties which are above and beyond looking after the people born in the time frame that I care for, and this is a labor of love."

"Ieiazel, I remember one of the first times we spoke you told me what you normally do in the heavenly realms, and you said that this was, '...to help relieve people from pain and suffering by performing miracles on earth by God's grace.'"

"Lee, I still carry out these duties. This is my life's work that I have chosen to do in God's heavenly kingdom. And when the days are over and my duties are far less we will rejoice together and bathe in the beauty of the word, which is God. And we will bask in his glory and be at one with Him, and be at one with ourselves and the universe, once more."

"Once more, Ieiazel? Have we both 'been there and done that', before?"

"Lee, it is not the only time you and I have shared times together as in fact you are in spirit most of the time and you are here most of your life, and your life at the moment is merely a single speck of dust in the breeze.

"And you are to be re-united with me and my brethren very soon. We are to rejoice in this and we are to be grateful that we are here now to discuss this as we are very good friends.

"All those here who know you will remember you and they will want to join you, and they will want to bask in our sunshine and enjoy themselves; and all will want to know and ask you how to get to the level of higher learning in preparation for entering the God plane."

"I know they will be very interested in finding out as much as they can about the fifteen tests I had to pass to have direct access to Yahweh,

Chapter 5. House of Virtues.

Ieiazel, but what did you mean when you said, 'And you are to be re-united with me and my brethren very soon?' Do you mean to say that you think I will pass over very shortly?"

"Lee, I said what I had to say and I will leave it at that if you do not mind, as Father does not want to tell you yet. He will tell you Himself or you will find out for yourself, sooner or later."

"Okay, I was only wondering if 'soon' meant before or after Judgment Day starts, as I am told this is only around the corner now, and if it is before judgment starts, then that means I will be in spirit again very soon, doesn't it?"

"Lee, it does, but do not worry as it will only be a temporary arrangement and you will be back on earth again soon afterwards."

"Temporary arrangement? Well, that sounds very, very strange to me Ieiazel; now, what can you tell me about your recreation time if you have any?"

"Lee, my duties are also my leisure if you know what I mean and I want to mention now that we need to do a few things for later on. We can both do these things together which will be to put in place a new set of rules to cover the New World Order[11] after the judgment is over, then we can get the house in order again once the commotion has died down."

"It looks like we'll both be very busy then Ieiazel! Thank you for your time and your comments and I'll speak to you about this later, as I'm already writing down these new rules ready for the New World Order in Yahweh's 'last word and testament.' Goodbye for now my friend."

"Lee, goodbye: take care as you need to finish this work soon, so rest now and take it easy."

---

[11] This New World Order will be run by the Nine Houses of Angels, not by politicians.

House of Powers

Guardian angels residing in this house look after those born
- 14th October to 22nd November -

God says, "The angels in my House of Powers are the ones I send to look into matters of life and death. These angels also keep the earth plane in order and make the demons behave themselves."

HAHAHEL -   looks after those born on 14th October to 18th October.

"Hello Hahahel, would you mind spending a few minutes with me to answer some questions?"
"Not at all Lee, go ahead and ask as many questions as you like."
"First of all, are you Hahahel, an angel from the House of Powers?"
"Yes, it is me and I am from the House of Powers!"
"Thanks, what do you do there, Hahahel?"
"Lee, my time is spent looking into the lives of those in spirit and schooling them for their next incarnation. I make them aware of any short-comings they have and the pitfalls they may face. They are going into a physical realm once more and although I tell them that the body is frail and it is not a very long life-span, they still want to do it.

"They have their reasons and they feel that the life they are going to have will be an exciting adventure. They feel that the life they are going to have will be full of love, children, surprises and earthly things to enjoy.

"They want to feel the sunshine and the rain; feel the summer heat and the winter cold, feel the taste of all things and ask that God look after them. And they ask for parents to provide for them until they are on their own two feet."

Chapter 6. House of Powers.

"But some want everything they see, and they want even more than that; they want power over each other, they want money; they want sex and want the best of food and clothing, as well."

"Well, I can understand why you're schooling them then, Hahahel; what do you do in your free time?"

"Lee, I go to the earth plane and I ask those in spirit if they would like to get out of there. And they say, 'Of course we would!' and I say to them, 'Well, you didn't think of that before you made fools of yourselves and sinned, did you? And now look at you!'"

"And what else do you do Hahahel?"

"Lee, I tell them that unless they change for the better, they cannot become light beings again and will remain here in hell; and they say, 'Who cares!' and I say, 'You will one day, when Father calls you to account for the dreadful lives you have led!

"And you will be in a state of fear and trembling! And you will wish you had been good and had never heard of the earth, and had never succumbed to a wicked life, which is sinful! We know all about you!

"And we are here to tell you that you can be saved if you are good! And we are monitoring your appalling behavior just in case you decide to turn over a new leaf and behave yourselves!

"Then we will review you and we will make you do some tasks to test you! And if you pass these tests then we will reconsider you when the time of judgment is upon you! We will consider the results of these tests, and we will be able to determine the fate that awaits you, and we will decide what to do with you then!'"

"Do you speak to these spirits individually or in a group, Hahahel?"

"Lee, it is in a classroom and they sit about taking notes, listening to my words of wisdom; wishing I was out of there leaving them alone, and

Chapter 6. House of Powers.

they wish they were not being taken to task. They complain and they groan and they moan but they know that I turn a deaf ear to it.

"And unless I am satisfied with them they will remain here unless another messenger arrives to rescue them from the fate that awaits them. They realize that unless they are saved from here they will perish in the pit. And they have no means of turning over a new leaf here in hell, as they are in the waiting room and are frightened really, but what can I do?

"The other thing is that most of them have family members here with them and some of them will refuse to leave them behind even if they are forgiven. And they will refuse to leave them, even if it means they will also go to the pit and suffer the second death."

"Hahahel, if some are forgiven and go to the light, won't they become very upset knowing that some of their friends and relatives they are going to leave behind are going to perish, after judgment?"

"Lee, this is the difficult part as most people have had many lives and most of them have been good, but if their most recent life has been bad and unforgivable, then they are to be discarded and will perish.

"The people left to live forever will always remember them and this is part of our universal existence. The people who have lived many lives will have many loved ones remaining with them, and they will find happiness beyond the happiness they had known in their life on earth."

"Hahahel, if a person willfully murders someone after having lived, say ten consecutive lives, do the previous good lives count for anything when it is time for judgment?"

"Yes Lee, *if* this sinner is forgiven at the time of judgment then he or she will go to the light, but not enter God's house."

"Thanks, Hahahel, I'll leave it there for now and say goodbye."

"Lee, goodbye and remember to keep in contact with me!"

Chapter 6. House of Powers.

MIKAEL - looks after those born on 19th October to 23rd October.

"Hello Mikael, it's Lee; do you have a few minutes free to speak to me about your role in the house and tell me what you do, and how you spend your spare time, if and when you get any?"

"Lee! Am I glad to hear from you! It has been many, many years my friend. I am overjoyed at this opportunity to speak to you again, and after this interview is finished I want to chat for an hour or two if I may, as we have an awful lot of catching up to do."

"Certainly Mikael, are you the angel Mikael from the House of Powers?"

"Lee, that is who I am, the one and the same! Please let me help you with this writing as I am an excellent scribe. My whole life has been one of writing and my whole career if you can call it that is one of reading and writing.

"My whole calling is to keep the stories of the day in the record books so that we can look at them whenever it is necessary to remember the full details, and we reminisce over these records and pull them out to teach others the right and the wrong way of it all.

"We show all the deceased these records of their past-lives to refresh their memories, and they are intrigued as many have not remembered most of the small details as they have had so many lives, that they merge into one.

"They are sad and they are happy as they remember the things they did. And they shout with glee and cry with shame, and all are shown these records to make them aware of why they are where they are, and the truth is in these records!"

"So Lee, what are you doing now?"

Chapter 6. House of Powers.

(I spoke to Mikael for nearly two hours discussing what I was up to and other various topics of interest.)

"Lee, what an interesting life you have!"

"Thanks Mikael, but like everybody else, I've had my moments!"

"Lee, I am so happy to hear from you again that I am nearly bursting and I will tell you more about some of my experiences later.

"If you like you can write a few books about these as I have the records of millions of people here and the stories cannot be matched by any other authority, as it is the only truthful record of what has transpired.

"I have them here for you to look at, at any time and you are quite welcome to see them. I would like to show you the records of people who you have not known but have been in the limelight, and you will be shocked at their behavior, as you can well imagine!"

"Thanks for the offer, Mikael. If I ever take up a career as a writer I'll let you know. Then we can write some very interesting stories based on the hitherto unobtainable information that you so eagerly want to provide me with, straight from the Angelic Records." [12]

"Lee, the records go back to the start and the history is fascinating! You may recall the ancient library in Alexandria, Egypt? It was destroyed several times as the successive conquering oppressors did not agree with the old ways and wanted all to learn new ways.

"They burnt nearly all of the records available then, except for a few valuable manuscripts which were stolen away and saved for posterity that have now been recovered and studied."

"Yes Mikael, I've heard about that tragic saga when all the valuable knowledge of the ages was lost. The conquerors also imposed their own

---

[12] A record of all past and present lives.

Chapter 6. House of Powers.

cultures and ideas onto the people."

"Lee, this knowledge is all here to be looked at and all has been recorded for you to look at whenever you want to!"

"Thank you for the wonderful offer Mikael, please remind me about this later on... and now, do you mind if I ask what you do when you have some spare time to yourself?"

"Lee, I go and visit my friends who are in other realms and are not from one of the houses of angels. My friends are in the spiritual realms as I have known many fine people and I like to keep in touch with them whenever possible.

"They love to hear my voice and they look forward to seeing me as much as I look forward to seeing them."

"Well thank you for that, Mikael. I'll say goodbye for now and speak to you again later, goodnight."

"Goodnight Lee, and remember to contact me again soon!"

"Lee, may I interrupt?"

"Who is it?"

"Lee, it is Mikael again!"

"Are you Mikael, the angel from the House of Powers?"

"Yes, Lee, and I want to say how happy I am to see you again."

(Only a night has passed since I last spoke to Mikael in our interview.)

"Thanks Mikael, I know you've known me for many, many years during my past-lives, but in this life I have no recollection of our prior friendship. Are you going to tell me more about it now, or would you like to add some more information to our interview?"

"Lee, I need to explain the previous conversation between you and the angel Ieiazel."

Chapter 6. House of Powers.

"Oh, okay! I must admit I'm a little curious about that... and have been wondering what's in store for me."

"Lee, you will not die then as you know it. Your conscious mind will be replaced with a temporary 'walk-in' from one of your past-lives now stored within your higher-self." [13]

"What? – Why is it necessary for me to change over from my present life? – Why is one of my past-life selves taking over my present life? Most of my past-life memories stored within my higher-self will be out of date for this day and age anyway, wont they?"

"Lee, they are and because you live in this day and age and your higher-self has lived in other times, we need your present-self in the spiritual realms to take part in a very important meeting with God and his most trusted servants. We will also take the opportunity to show you our nine houses, as we did with John."[14]

"Mikael, past-life memories are stored and remain with the higher-self as well as being written down and recorded in the Angelic Records, aren't they?"

"Yes Lee, we know all of the lives you have had and you will know as well, as all of your past-life memories are reinstated into your living memory at the time of judgment, to be judged on the Day of Judgment."

"Okay! Let's go over this Mikael, this walk-in will definitely be a past-life from my higher-self, won't it, and not any other spirit entity trying to barge in, taking over?"

---

[13] A human life can be compared to a memory stick and a life memory the information stored on it. At death, each life memory is stored on the permanent hard disk drive of your personal computer (your higher self) and can be retrieved and reviewed later. Your soul is akin to the central processing unit of the computer and your spirit, the power driving it.

[14] See (Revelation 4:2)

Chapter 6. House of Powers.

"Let me tell you now that a walk-in is provided by Father! Not an unauthorized possession by an unclean spirit that would result in problems! This is to be for your benefit, not to your detriment! The walk-in entering your body will be from a small part of your higher-self that makes up all of you. Father wants to have you here to show you the spiritual realms, to tutor you in spiritual matters as well as hear your opinion and listen to your views. This is to bring about a complete picture seen from the eyes of a living person, who is seeing and hearing the results of human deeds firsthand."

"I see! And Yahweh decided to let you tell me this now?"

"Yes, He summoned me before Him and asked me to give you the complete details, as otherwise you may feel anxious and think you are going to be called home and leave your loved ones prematurely. He wants me to tell you this will not be your time, as you are to be returned after your mission is completed."

"Okay, thanks Mikael. What you're telling me sounds incredible! I've heard about walk-ins before, but not a walk-in from a past-life memory as a mind replacement though. Demonic possession is different from this and some cases of possession I've heard about have created multiple personality disorders, wreaking havoc with the life of the person being taken over, as two or more souls share the body at the same time, with both or all of them fighting for control.

"So... apparently, I'll be vacating to let a part of my higher-self take over; and if it's one of my previous lives from my higher-self temporarily looking after my present body, I shouldn't have too much to worry about, as hopefully I will be in good hands."

"Lee, the situation should be regarded as a temporary vacation from your body and you will have an experience that is unique in this day and age. Your life will be changed from then on as you will have firsthand

Chapter 6. House of Powers.

knowledge of the heavenly realms and you can tell the faithful about it on your return."

"Hmmm... I don't know if anyone will believe this Mikael! I'll just have to wait and see."

"Lee, it is going to be alright. Trust us, as we trust you to do a very good job."

"Do you think this walk-in phenomenon we're discussing should be included as part of our interview Mikael, or do you think it will be too weird to include and best be left out and kept confidential, at least for now?"

"Lee, by all means write this in our book as it will arouse interest. Let all that read this realize that we can replace the soul of the living with the soul of another if need be, and that the soul can be replaced at will by Father. Sometimes evil spirits and demons left on the earth plane try this and possess a person who has problems in their life, so then, that person is thought to be insane."

"What happens to these possessed people, Mikael?"

"The demon either drives the possessed person to suicide or we step in and help through an experienced messenger, psychic or priest who performs an exorcism, and that intruder is then expelled from the living body by being ordered out."

"Okay, I can understand that and then what happens to the intruding entity?"

"Father has it destroyed immediately as it has broken the rules and it is punishable by the second death. Possession of another is one of the few times Father has Meheliah, the Angel of Death, extinguish a soul He creates, before the time of judgment."

Chapter 6. House of Powers.

"Thank you for coming back with this information Mikael and it will be an eye-opener for some, especially those with no prior knowledge in these matters, and I appreciate it!"

"Lee, I was going to tell you, Father originally wanted to tell you Himself when the time was at hand, but it has served its purpose now by giving the people who read this a look at another dimension of their lives that otherwise would not have been known to them."

"Like nearly everything else inspired by the angels in this book, Mikael."

"Yes Lee, goodbye for now."

"Lee, it is Father!"

"Hello Yahweh, are you God, creator of all heaven and earth?"

"Yes Lee, it is coming along very well and I am very pleased with you. And I am very happy to see you talking to all the guardian angels. And I am very pleased with the information as all is accurate. And it is my wish to have it published soon and all will be taken care of so do not concern yourself with it. And it will be finished before the end of the year. So put your mind to it and I will have you writing another book for me next year, as foretold."

"Alright Father, I will speak to you about it later on, thank you."

"Let it remain we must let all have this knowledge before the time of judgment, to let all believers take the necessary steps to save themselves, and from their ever having to have the agony of the second death imposed upon their souls. And it will be the beginning of a wonderful life without hindrance of any kind."

"Yes Yahweh, all believers should certainly start taking measures."

Chapter 6. House of Powers.

VEULIAH -   looks after those born on 24th October to 28th October.

"Hello Veuliah, may I speak to you; that is, if you have a few minutes to spare?"

"Lee, it is Veuliah; it will be a pleasure to spend some of my time with you!"

"Are you Veuliah, an angel from the House of Powers?"

"Yes I am and I have been waiting eagerly to meet you!"

"Thank you Veuliah, I'm very pleased to meet you, too."

"Lee, I am the Angel of Mercy and I give my time trying to save those who are dying from any cause. I try to save them if possible and give them all the encouragement they need to return to their body. And even when they resist, I still give them this opportunity."

"Well, that *is* very good of you Veuliah, very noble indeed!"

"Lee, thank you for your encouragement; I feel that it is doing some good to help them return as they may have been taken by accident or murder, and I still find it distressing, to see people being hurt.

"I feel it is my duty to resuscitate them if possible as it gives me great satisfaction to be able to save someone who has died and then return them to life."

"Does it help you if they have an earthly messenger calling them back as well, Veuliah?"

"Yes it does help Lee, and sometimes when I have arrived too late a messenger has already been able to get them to return and they have survived, even after an extended period of death. Their soul has been hovering about on the earth plane waiting for their spirit guides to take them to the light, or leave them here in hell. If an earthly messenger asks them to return, they sometimes do, as they are not sure who is who and take the advice given to them from the messenger. And when the earthly

Chapter 6. House of Powers.

messenger is authorized by Father, the soul is compelled to return whether it wants to or not as there is no alternative, but to return."

"Well, this will be very interesting information for some people, Veuliah; and just how many earthly messengers are here on earth that Yahweh has authorized to do this?"

"Lee, I do not know how many earthly messengers are here, but I do know for certain that they are here and that they are here to do this. They are here to show the way to the light for many and they are to be the future leaders at the time of judgment, and they are the ones who will give hope to many. They are the ones who will show the multitudes their healing powers and they are to show the multitudes great miracles in the flesh. They are to give a much-needed boost of faith to the people who will see the works of our Father, as they have been anointed by Father to do His work."

"Veuliah, just what sort of miracles can we expect to see then, especially after the Messiah is back on earth with us once more?"

"Lee, the dead will be raised, the blind will see, the deaf will hear, the lame will walk, illnesses and diseases will be cured, afflictions will be fixed; even those followers with Aids will be cured!"

"Will any be cured who are not Christians and do not acknowledge that the Son of Man is the Son of God?"

"Lee, if they believe in Him at the time, they will be cured!"

"It sounds as if the human race is in for a miraculous time ahead then, Veuliah!"

"Lee, I will be looking forward to it and I am going to help Jesus as much as I can!"

"I'm sure He will appreciate your help, Veuliah! What can you tell me about your personal life and what do you do in your spare time?"

Chapter 6. House of Powers.

"I look after the young people who are at risk of overdosing and I watch them to see if they are going to die or not and keep them alive until the medical team arrives, or they are over it. And if they are overdosed and die on the drugs, I save them and I say to them, 'For goodness sake, do not do that again!' But they do! And if they die again I do not bother with them as they will just do it over again!"

"It is better to let them die and stay on the earth plane in spirit where they cannot bother people and where they will wish they had been more productive with the life they have wasted. And addicts will be punished for wasting their lives, so if you know of any, then always remember to ask Father to forgive them!"

"Okay Veuliah, thank you very much for your time and patience as I've had numerous interruptions whilst speaking to you, and you have been very patient waiting for me to finish. I appreciate it very much. Goodbye for now and I hope to speak to you again shortly."

"Lee, thank you too, goodbye!"

YELAHIAH - looks after those born on 29th October to 2nd November.

"Lee, it is Yelahiah!"

"Hello Yelahiah, are you an angel from the House of Powers?"

"Lee, it is Yelahiah, and yes, I reside in the House of Powers."

"Thanks Yelahiah, can you give me any idea of the role you play in the heavenly realms?"

"Lee, I have an important role here and I do not like to be referred to as someone playing my role as I have important work, and it is not a game to me!"

"Okay Yelahiah, – well, this is just a figure of speech we use and its meaning is the same as asking you what sort of work you do."

Chapter 6. House of Powers.

"Lee, it is a silly figure of speech and I dislike it when people say one thing and mean another. You must be running for public office, the way you say these things!"

"Yelahiah, this is ridiculous! I see the funny side of this at the moment and you probably know I have little time for most politicians; are you playing a joke on me?"

"Yes Lee, I was jesting and I am the angel who takes our Father visiting to the heavenly realms. I am His personal advisor and whenever He wants to see who a particular spirit being is, when a friend or relative prays for them, He asks me to pinpoint that spirit and I do.

"He then asks me to bring that spirit before Him and asks me to bring an account of their past lives before Him. Then He asks me to give Him the scrolls to read and He forgives those who are prayed for and asks me to escort them away again. Then He also gets me to change their scrolls to show who it was that asked for forgiveness on their behalf, as nothing at all is missed.

"And even the ant you walk on is written down in the records, and even the very last words you utter are written in the scrolls, and all is kept to look at for when the time of judgment is here. And I believe it will be here soon and the last days will be upon us all, and the world will become unbearable.

"Soon the world will become even more wicked and sinful than it is now, as all of those with no morals will become like wild animals in the wilderness, tearing each other to shreds. And all will wail and all will be fearful. And this is the time prior to judgment. And those who are listening will, and those who are not listening, will not."

"Yelahiah, you are most likely on first name terms with our Father as you know Him very well and are with Him constantly. How do you manage to get away if you have to attend to people, and do your duty as

Chapter 6. House of Powers.

their personal guardian angel in the time frame allocated to you, to look after them in?"

"Lee, I ask Father for leave, as He informs me where to go and who to help. He informs us all of our duties and He gives out the scrolls every day. We do these duties and in an emergency He dispatches us to help immediately, and there is a proper sequence of events to follow.

"We are well drilled so that in the event of a major catastrophe we are ready to escort the souls to the realms they belong to. We counsel them and we look after them until they are settled. And we always give them the opportunity to do whatever they need to do before the gates are shut. And they are unable to go from one realm to the next by themselves without asking, and without escort.

"The spirits are well versed in the rules and they are given many pleasant tasks to do to keep them fully occupied without boring them, and the amount and the variety of duties they carry out is much more than on earth, so they are constantly busy.

"They are happy here and they are all friendly toward each other, and as for those in spirit left on the earth plane, most are not as well off as they are here, but they exist in a manner which is not too uncomfortable except for the emotional burden they carry."

"Well, that's a lot of information Yelahiah, and lately each angel seems to be giving me just a little more information than the last."

"Lee, it is normal to try to give more than the last as this is how we operate here. All giving just a little more of ourselves than the one who went before and this keeps us competitive and makes us happy too. I am needed at home now, so will bid you goodbye."

"I see; well thank you for your contribution and I'll go on to the next interview. Goodbye for now, Yelahiah."

Chapter 6. House of Powers.

SEHALIAH - looks after those born on 3rd November to 7th November.

"Hello Sehaliah, may I speak to you if you have a spare minute?"

"Lee, it is Sehaliah, and yes, I can spend half an hour or more with you, if you like."

"Are you Sehaliah, an angel from the House of Powers?"

"Yes Lee, it is, and I will spend my time here with you, for as long as you need."

"Thank you; are you aware of what I'm going to ask you about? I would like to have some information about your role as a guardian angel and also have some information about your leisure time."

"Lee, my role is that of one of the messengers who gives the faithful believers their serve of faith, and I give them inspiration and strength to keep on going, under all circumstances.

"When things on earth look bleak, and the droughts; fires, famines and floods wreak havoc with their lives; and the Aids epidemic and other plagues hit people who are vulnerable, I give them uplifting words that Father asks me to convey to them. I pass these messages on to them and they are made to feel much better, as they know that I am telling them encouraging words from our Father, who does these things for a purpose.

"When things look bleak to us, He is not bleak but is planning the next step, and He is thinking ahead about the progression to be made from a disaster that is terrible in the eyes of the people. And to Father, it is part of the forthcoming events, and it gives Him purpose to create more and to improve on the earth.

"He allows these natural disasters to let us rally together and to learn that death is part of life and that to lose a loved one is part of life. And to cry and to weep and to feel devastated is to use the emotions we are

Chapter 6. House of Powers.

capable of using, that He gave us; and to feel deeply hurt is to fully use the emotions that He gave us.

"Don't you think that if you did not cry when you were feeling devastated, it would seem abnormal? And if you laughed when you were in the throes of agony, would it not seem strange? And if you were unable to fully express your feelings then you would not be a complete person.

"So do not think it wrong to laugh when others are happy or to cry when they are unhappy, as each has their own life to lead!

"Each person has their own emotions and each must learn to live with the events that happen. If you are taken by one of these disasters, then you will be back home earlier than planned, but it is part of the overall destiny and it will be part of your overall life.

"It will make you more aware as it will be another part of you. It will help you understand that all is ongoing, and all has no end except the end Father has in mind. And no-one is to know that end and it is to be the end of the world as it is now.

"During the Day of Judgment when our Father is ridding us of all the rubbish, we will be able to live in peace without fear of people turning against us or bombing us or stealing from us, or any of the dreadful things that humans do to each other now.

"And only those who want love and want to live in peace will, and all those who do not will perish, as it is part of Father's plan to do this.

"Lee, it is to be the end of the world for people who are not to be saved and I am going to be there watching to make sure it is carried out with precision as I want it all to end properly, without any of those who have created trouble here. They do not have the right to be here to destroy the world again! And I am going to make certain that they are sent to the ends of the earth, and I am going to ask Father to let me be

Chapter 6. House of Powers.

one of the angels who is to destroy them as I have seen these wicked people in action, and I hate them with a vengeance!

"I will enjoy seeing them at the time of retribution, seeing them pay for their misdeeds; and I would like to add that all of us want to see it, as we have had to watch each of them do their unholy deeds.

"We have all just had to sit back and watch and we are going to be there to condemn them, and we are going to make sure none escape and we will tell them this! And we are all going to watch as they writhe and scream in agony! And we are all going to watch as they suffer the fate they gave others to suffer! And we will all rejoice in this!

"And we will ask them, 'Why do you cry?' And they will say, 'Because we burn!' And we will ask, 'Why don't you ask Father to tell you why you burn?' And they will respond by asking, 'What did we do wrong?' And then we will bring out the records to show them.

"And they will be in a state of emotional pain and anxiety, suffering more than anyone can imagine, as they cannot perish until Father has had His pleasure, watching them suffer.

"And all that have suffered at their hands will rejoice! And all that have been wronged will be overjoyed! And all there wringing their hands will be in the throes of an agonizing death! Then, and only then, after they have paid for all of their sins will they perish! Never to return and never to trouble us, and never ever to be part of us; or to be with us, or be seen by us; or to be heard of by us, ever again!

"And they will be forgotten as the dust that is wiped off our boots is forgotten! And they will be forgotten as the dirt that is swept out of the door is forgotten! And hopefully they will never be thought of again and be forgotten! And we will all be overjoyed at the prospect of a perfect world where peace will reign!"

Chapter 6. House of Powers.

"All will be happy and all will have plenty! And there will be sharing and there will be an abundance to go around! And no-one will hoard anything like a little squirrel! And no-one will keep things to themselves like a little rodent! And no-one will have any reason to hide anything! And all will be spoken in front of the other and not behind the back of the other! And all will be laid on the table without being hidden under the table!"

"Well! That was a quite a lot to say, Sehaliah and thank you for your contribution. Now that you've vented all that out of your system, would you like to tell me about any of the activities you enjoy in your leisure time?"

"Yes my friend! I go about the universe watching the way it has developed and how it is so peaceful and how it is now so wonderful without the hot steaming gases that used to be. The first signs of primitive life have now evolved into much more developed life forms, and humans have progressed from the primitives they were when Father first created them to where they are now in less than a few thousand years.

"This is amazing to me as before that, I remember when they roamed about as nomads, foraging for food and searching for something to eat in the forests. And I remember this as being not too long ago!

"And now they are wearing beautiful clothes, driving beautiful cars and living in beautiful dwellings! And life for some is wonderful!

"And now they say, 'Other people can go to hell, as they do not matter! They do not deserve to share in this as they are not known to us! They are from another country and are lesser beings!'

"But in the eyes of Father, Father created each of us as equals in His eyes and His children are all loved by Him. And He expects people to look after each other, not turn a blind eye to their plights and misfortunes."

Chapter 6. House of Powers.

"Thanks for all of that information, Sehaliah; I had better leave it there as I still have many of the other angels waiting to speak to me. Goodbye for now and I would like to thank you for your contribution."

"Lee, please do not go yet as I would like to add a few more details!"

"Okay then, I guess it's alright, as while you're here and you have more to say then it's still a part of the interview, isn't it?"

"Yes of course it is, Lee, and I want to say that the people who are going to be in charge at the time of judgment will be fair. And they will be able to distribute food and clothing and provide shelter to those remaining on earth. They will take control, and for the first time in history people will feel safe and people will be looked after and they will go about without any fear. And the people will have no worries on their mind and will rejoice in the world.

"There will be sharing and they will be giving each other provisions and will not even have to worry about money, as all will be provided for by Father, who will provide all things to all people who ask Him."

"Sehaliah, has there ever been a judgment before, prior to this one pending?"

"Lee, it is not to be discussed in detail here; but yes, this judgment has passed over the earth before when Father flooded all and all perished except for a few He cherished. And He kept his promise then and He will keep his promise now!"

"So some of the people who were living then are already on the God plane? The people who were saved?"

"Lee, I have to tell you, except for a chosen few, none were saved and none have entered the God plane! And all those except a chosen few who lived then have been destroyed as Father started again."

"And the chosen ones that survived the flood have lived and died many times as you have. The souls of some of them are here in spirit

Chapter 6. House of Powers.

and the souls of some of them are on earth today in physical bodies they have chosen for themselves.

"And their descendants live in countries all over the world. And the ones who are in spirit are here to oversee their friends as they are usually guides for them, and I am overseeing them too."

"Thank you for telling me about your leisure time and your role in heaven, Sehaliah. Now, while you're still here can you tell me a little about how you spend your time in your own personal life?"

"Lee, my spare time is taken up playing my flute and I love to play the tunes that I hear, and I love to play my other instruments too. I have been playing these for thousands of years now and I am a perfectionist when it comes to playing instruments.

"I am going to tell you that few can play as well as I can as I have been practicing; and they ask me to show them how to play. And I ask them if they are prepared to spend time each and every day practicing, otherwise they will not be any good, as to play properly is a joy that can only be realized by those few musicians who strive for perfection."

"Thank you for that extra snippet of information, Sehaliah; I'll bid you farewell for now, and I'll try to speak to you again as soon as possible; goodbye."

"Lee, I would like to add that another thing I do here is to provide the other angels with my undying devotion. They know my music is for them and that is the reason I play it, for their ears, as it is not the same as playing it and listening; the listener usually enjoys it much more than those singing it or playing it."

"I can relate to that, Sehaliah; thank you again and goodbye."

"Goodbye Lee, the others you have interviewed earlier now tell me they wish they had told you much more!"

"Thank you, Sehaliah; perhaps next time, goodbye."

Chapter 6. House of Powers.

ARIEL -   looks after those born on 8th November to 12th November.

"I would like to speak to Ariel, an angel from the House of Powers!"

"Lee, it is Ariel, and yes I am an angel of the Lord God and I am an angel of the heavens, and I live in the House of Powers!"

"Hello Ariel, thank you for coming, I'm very pleased to meet you. What I would like from you is a brief summary of your heavenly duties and a short description of your personal life, with perhaps a little about your hobbies, if you don't mind?"

"Lee, my duties are to bring about change and I do. I make the people look at what they are doing from a different angle and I make them think, 'It is time to move, or it is time to make some changes here. It is time to replace the car, or it is time to get married, it is time for me to go to school again, or time to make a change in my career.'

"I encourage this as it makes the world go round and I oversee these changes, as I want all to move. And all the people must change otherwise nothing would ever be different and nobody would buy anything, and no-one would sell anything and all would come to a standstill.

"And so I give them the ideas that enter into their minds, and I give them the incentive to go out and make something happen. I give them the ideas that are needed to change things. And even if they only change their minds, it is my influence. I am the one who makes change and I am the one responsible for change as I have been asked to do this by Father, and I do it!

"My hobbies? I change them from day to day, as I want to encourage the other angels to keep on the move, too. My main love is the flute and I play a different tune each time. My hobbies also include playing the

Chapter 6. House of Powers.

drums as I like them too, though sometimes I like the violin as well, and I play a whole range of musical instruments.

"I go from one house to another, encouraging angels to change their attitude toward the spirits, keeping them in the throes of indecision until they have made up their minds, just to change them again. And I will keep on changing things until the end as without change nothing progresses. Even if the change is for the worse it is better in my eyes as a change for the worse is better than no change at all."

"Ariel, what was that you said? A change for the worse is better than no change at all?"

"Lee, you do not understand?"

"No, not really and I for one dislike constant change as I find it too disruptive. For instance, a friend is constantly moving; changing her address from one place to another and frankly it drives me crazy with all the unnecessary work and worry she creates."

"Lee, that is not the point! The point is to move on so that others move and this causes a chain reaction, as one move starts a hundred moves that never stop, as each place vacated has to be filled! And this movement creates employment and that is what puts the bread and butter on the table! So the changes I bring about are to create employment! And even if you change the color of your boat or your bicycle it creates employment for dozens of people who make the paints and the brushes, the air compressors and the hoses; the spray guns and the spray booths, and the factory buildings! The costs are included in the product bringing the total cost to the people and it is distributed among the people, who all have steady employment!"

"Thank you Ariel, have you anything more to say?"

"Yes! It is not the fault of the messenger that problems are created, but the way people go about change! I excuse myself from your

Chapter 6. House of Powers.

accusation of me creating problems for people! It is for the betterment of humanity and I will justify my work! And I will tell the people that without me nothing would be moved and nothing would be built! And all things would remain the same and the people would be lazy! And they would not have anything to do except eat and sleep and they would find this life unbearable! And they would find it not to their liking! And it is for the advancement of the human race that I do my work!"

"Okay, okay, I see! Thank you Ariel; goodbye for now and I would like to speak to you again later on."

"Lee, please forgive my brusque attitude as it comes across as very negative and I do not want to portray myself in this light. Would you please delete it all and start over?"

"Pardon me, Ariel? I think your interview was very informative and to delete it would be a dreadful waste. I think it would be much better just to have another interview following on from here if you want to and then all the insights you have given us already will not be lost."

"Lee, are you sure?"

"Definitely, Ariel; it would be a waste of time and energy to delete any of this. Would you like to start again?"

"Alright, Lee; my duties are to create change and I do this with the people's workings and the people's prosperity in mind. This is over all things they do and includes the emotional and physical changes they experience. My job is to ensure that the world progresses through an avalanche of goods being consumed and renewed.

"The changes I bring about are all to do with human needs and I do these things to help with life's daily routine. Without change, nothing would progress. I feel that my duties are extremely important for the progression of the human race and I feel that my contribution is invaluable. And I feel that without change, things such as the economy

Chapter 6. House of Powers.

would stagnate, and this is why I try to promote consumer confidence in new products."

"Thank you very much Ariel, that should suffice. The people reading this should now be aware of how important your work is, keeping the wheels of progress well oiled; goodbye for now."

"Goodbye, Lee, and it has been a pleasure to let all know how I think and feel about my divine work."

ASALIAH- looks after those born on 13th November to 17th November.

"Are you there, Asaliah? I would like to get a duty statement from you and a little information about your private life too, if that's possible?"

"Hello Lee, it is Asaliah, and how are you today?"

"I am well thanks, and how are you? Are you Asaliah from the House of Powers?"

"Yes Lee, I too am well and my duties entail watching over the people who are in prison. I watch them night and day by going from one prison to another, to hear those praying to Father. Father instructs me to go and console them and sometimes I answer their prayers if they are praying for something that can be fixed immediately.

"I give them hope and I give them love and I give them all the help that I can under the circumstances. And if they are despondent I cheer them up and I say to them that there is nothing to worry about, as all is even in the long run and they are to be judged by God, not by man.

"And those who incarcerate them will also be judged, as they are men and not gods! They are to be on the same playing field as the others at the time of judgment! I tell them these things and I tell them that in the long run the prisoners will be the warders and the warders will be the prisoners, depending upon the circumstances!"

Chapter 6. House of Powers.

"And I say to them, 'Do not be overwrought as all is for your own growth, and all will be explained at a higher level. You are here because it is seen to be a lesson for you to learn!' And even those in prison who are totally innocent have a lot to learn as they have put others in prison previously and now they pay with their time.

"And all of those who mistreat prisoners will be mistreated by ten times! And all that take advantage of them will suffer intolerable anguish and they will have to beg to be forgiven! And I make certain that all these things are recorded!

"From years ago to the present everything that has ever been spoken and everything that has ever been done is on record! And I would emphasize that those among you who do not have a friend or relative in prison will one day know what prisoners go through!"

"Asaliah, you say that the innocent in prison are paying for putting others in prison previously. Were these others also innocent? And do all people who put others in prison have to pay for this, later on?"

"Lee it is not to be taken literally as it is a euphemism for those who mistreat others by being unfair in their judgments and being harsh in ways that are seen as unacceptable.

"Though not bad enough to be excluded from the light, it has been a tarnish on their record, and they go through this anguish now rather than later on after judgment as it is to be redressed either then or now, and they are placed here in prison by their spirit guides who feel it is best to pay now rather than later, when all will be rejoicing.

"And the reason for this is so that they will all be in the middle of the times of retribution with joy on their faces rather than distress."

"Now, how will we know what other prisoners go through, Asaliah?"
"Lee, you are all to be judged on the Day of Judgment and all will be

Chapter 6. House of Powers.

called to account! And all will have to go through anxiety that is in proportion to your sins, until it is decided how you have to pay!"

"So, are you are saying that those in the spirit world are akin to being in prison?"

"Those deceased souls left on the earth plane are indeed in prison until judgment is passed upon them!"

"The spirits in the light are also to be judged but have the knowledge that they will not perish, as souls left on the earth plane may well perish! And those in the light will be judged and placed accordingly, on the level they have reached.

"The system is very similar here to the way people choose to treat each other in life, and they have chosen this way for themselves, following tradition."

"Thank you Asaliah, now can you briefly tell me what you do in your free time?"

"My life is very pleasing and I find a lot of good in people, even those in prison! And some are Christians, some devout Catholics and Protestants; some are Jews and some are from the Muslim faith and many are from other religions and sects.

"My hobby is to differentiate between their beliefs and traditions, then I can tell Father who in their midst is following the rules that they have made for themselves and who isn't.

"But really, in the end, all it means is that those who believe in Father and the Son will have more chance than those who do not. So I give Father the balance of the scales at the time they die to see whether or not they are worthy to be in the light. And this is measured on their behavior, not on their religion!"

"Okay, thank you Asaliah; goodbye."

"Goodbye Lee, please stay in touch with me."

Chapter 6. House of Powers.

MIHAEL -   looks after those born on 8th November to 22nd November.

"Mihael, do you have a moment or two free to speak to me?"
"Hello Lee, do you want to interview me now?"
"Yes Mihael, are you an angel from the House of Powers?"
"I am, and let it be that my words are written down for all to see!"

♫ *"I am the angel Mihael, who transports the souls of the dead,*
And if they're not quite ready, I sing and play the harp instead.
♪ *I take the souls of all the dead, to the ends of mother earth,* ♪
And put them in their proper place, with lots of fun and mirth.

♫ *"And from way on high in the big blue sky, I look upon their graves,*
And at all their friends and neighbors, betwixt the other knaves. ♪
♪ *I give those souls left in Hades, as much time as they need with any,*
And the company is quite uncanny, as the unholy dead are many." ♫

"What does that little ditty mean, Mihael? I was expecting to hold a deep and meaningful discussion with you, supposedly about your role of transporting souls of the dead and about the other angelic duties you perform on earth and in heaven, and *this* is what you come up with!"
"Lee, I am sorry if I have annoyed you with my light hearted jingle!"
"No, I'm not annoyed Mihael, it's just that you started off by singing about transporting the souls of the dead and it aroused my interest and raised my expectations. Is this transport to take the deceased souls from the earth plane to their respective levels in the light?"
"Lee, my role is to deliver the souls of the dead to their allocated places. And I take them to school and I take them to choir-practice, and I take them to conferences and I take them to major events."

Chapter 6. House of Powers.

♪ *"And I take 'em here and I take 'em there and I take 'em every flamin' where!"* ♪

"Hmmm, I see! You escort souls of the dead to their respective levels and to their many appointments Mihael. How many levels in the spiritual realms do you work on?"

"Lee, I work on all the levels in the light but I do not bother with those evil spirits left on the earth plane after I leave them there, as they are incapable of seeing or hearing anything there. What purpose is it to transport them anywhere when they are in the waiting room?"

"So you're saying that those deceased souls who are left on the earth plane simply mill about without any way of communicating, except by thought alone?"

"Yes Lee, they are orbs of energy and they cannot do any harm unless they attach themselves to a person and then they can see and hear. But the punishment for this is swift and they are dealt with summarily on the spot by Father who sends the Angel of Death and Darkness, known to us as the Archangel Meheliah, to deal with them."

"Angel of Death *and* Darkness?"

"Yes Lee, there are thousands upon thousands of angels as you know and not all have duties like us as we are guardian angels and messengers, whereas the others have different roles and death is a major role here and darkness is a major role too."

"I'll bet! So the Angel of Death and Darkness will deal with all those who are to die the second death at the time of judgment?"

"Yes Lee, his role is to destroy those evil spirits and demons unfit to live and his many helpers are ready to provide assistance too."

"Mihael, does the Angel of Death and Darkness have any dealings with Satan, as many think Satan is to destroy those left in the abyss?"

Chapter 6. House of Powers.

"No Lee, Satan is bound on the earth plane and he will not be summoned before Father until the Day of Judgment."

"Mihael, what about all the evil events happening on earth, isn't Satan responsible for these?"

"Lee, Satan is on the earth plane as all other evil spirits are and he can do little, apart from influencing the thoughts of the wicked ones"

"Mihael, I constantly hear people say that Satan is responsible for this and for that and tempts them, so who is responsible?"

"Lee, people are constantly blaming their misfortunes on Satan as his works, and truly even if he could do all these things, why would he? His falling out was with our Father and not with the people and he will not be able to do anything except communicate for another thousand years now; and he will be unable to do anything in the future either. He will perish the same as all the others will, who have not followed the rules Father has given us!" [15]

"Yahweh, may I speak to you?"

"Lee, it is Father!"

"Are you God, creator of heaven and earth?"

"Yes Lee, I am, and you want to ask me a question?"

"Yahweh, what is going to happen to Satan? Will he create a lot of trouble in the last days?"

"Satan will not create any more problems for me or for anyone, either here or on earth."

"Yahweh, why were we told that he would be let out of his prison to cause problems for all of us after a thousand years of Christ's reign?"

---

[15] See (Revelation 20:1-10)

Chapter 6. House of Powers.

"Lee, Satan has been shackled in chains and he cannot create any more problems for humanity. And you have been told this before! And you are now asking again?"

"Yahweh, I have been told before but I need to be absolutely certain about this and hear it again, from you. I want to have you tell the readers in your own words, as only you can."

"Lee, the truth is that Satan is not going to make trouble for any and the ones who are making trouble for you are your leaders, and they will be punished severely."

"Thank you, Yahweh and when I write your 'last word and testament' I will elaborate on your plans and let all know what is going to happen."

"Lee, the book will be finished soon and all will be able to read it and all will have the knowledge that I am providing for them. And all will have no doubt then, as I will give them sign after sign and they will watch out for these. And all my faithful will know it is a sign and those who do not know will wonder at these happenings!"

"Thank you, Yahweh. I will start writing your Word as soon as I am able to."

"Lee, I thank you and please do not leave out any of my words as all are important and all have meaning. And those who read will be able to understand. And all who understand will know that it is my word and not your word!"

"I'll only write in what you auto-type for me and will continue with my work now, Yahweh."

"Lee, yes, and I will help you with this work too."

"Thank you Yahweh, goodbye for now."

Chapter 6. House of Powers.

"Mihael, let's continue now if you don't mind?"

"Lee, I was saying Meheliah, the Angel of Death and Darkness, extinguishes those demons that possess people and he does this on the spot as soon as they are exorcised; and this is his role at the moment.

"And it is also the rule now that lowly souls and demons are to truthfully identify themselves to messengers when asked where they come from and not pretend to be from the light. Father has given Meheliah the authority to instantly extinguish any soul or demon who impersonates a spirit from the light by lying about their identity."

"Yes Mihael, possession and impersonation are the only times that these wicked souls (known as evil spirits); unclean spirits or demons can perish before the time of judgment, as Yahweh has mentioned this to me earlier."

"Correct Lee, and no other has the power to destroy what Father has created. Therefore, Meheliah, though not the highest ranking in heaven, is the most powerful archangel in heaven, being in charge of death."

"What is the Darkness that Meheliah is the angel of, Mihael?"

"This refers to the earth plane, Lee. Meheliah's spiritual realm is the earth plane and he constantly roams around looking for any evil spirits who have broken Father's golden rule and destroys them."

"Does this Angel of Death and Darkness take the lives of people living on earth too?"

"Lee, I do not know and I doubt it though he has this power as Father had him help another angel kill the first born of Egypt, for Moses.[16] His duties now are to monitor the evil spirits on the earth plane and not the living."

"Mihael, what do you do in your spare time?"

---

[16] See (Exodus 12:23-30)

Chapter 6. House of Powers.

"Lee, I watch the events that I escort the spirits to see and I stay and watch these events until they are finished; then I escort these spirits back to where I found them."

"Where you *found* them Mihael; do they have free reign to travel throughout the astral plane, or do you mean back to their respective levels?"

"Lee, I take them back to their respective levels in the light which are very much like the places on earth if you can relate to that and all spirits have somewhere to live. And all that are residing there have a reality as you do here on earth.

"This reality is a better place to be than on earth as all the living souls on earth are mixed with the good and the bad like a barrel of fruit that has been left to rot.

"And while the ones at the bottom are rotting away the fresh ones at the top are not affected, but unless those on the top are removed and cleansed, they will turn rotten too, unable to be saved!"

"Do you have any other hobbies you can tell me about, Mihael?"

"Lee, I am also one of the charioteers and I love to travel, and I am constantly going from one place to another with the other angels as a group. And we look at the world from where we are and we listen to the people, and we watch what the people are doing.

"We all talk about the events that are taking place and what we can do if this happens or that happens, and we enjoy just being here!"

"Thank you Mihael. I'm sorry for the constant interruptions, but the 'phone is ringing and other people are here, intermittently speaking to me while I'm working; so, goodbye for now."

"Lee I have enjoyed speaking to you; goodbye and God bless you!"

House of Principalities

Guardian angels residing in this house look after those born
- 23rd November to 31st December -

God says, "My angels in this house look after the religious orders on earth and also inspire the leaders to greatness. The religious leaders listen to these angels and I would like the world leaders to listen to them too."

VEHUEL - looks after those born on 23rd November to 27th November.

"Hello Vehuel, it's Lee, would you mind giving me a brief outline of your duties and a little information about yourself for this interview?"

"Lee, it is Vehuel, yes I am able to comply with this as I have heard about you; and my contribution is also worthy of seeing the light of day!"

"Certainly; are you Vehuel, an angel from the House of Principalities?"

"Yes, I am the angel who gives advice to the world leaders and the respective Popes. And I give advice to the Archbishop of Canterbury and other high profile leaders who have a lot of authority over the people, as far as religion is allowed to; especially in matters of birth control, sex before marriage and confidentiality in personal matters.

"Some leaders think they have the authority to tell the people how to behave, and they try to tell the people not to have sex before marriage; not to have children out of wedlock, not to have indiscriminate sexual encounters and not to use birth control. The people are supposed to listen in awe and they are supposed to follow their leader's advice; they are supposed to learn the laws of their religion and follow the ways of their church."

Chapter 7. House of Principalities

"Vehuel, what's your personal opinion on these matters of birth control, sex before marriage and having children out of wedlock then?"

"Lee, birth control is not my idea but there is no law against it and my Father does not complain about it, only some churches do as it affects the number of members they have, not the concern for the right for life. And this is the real reason for them being against it, even though protected sex also helps in the fight against Aids and other sexually transmitted diseases, saving many thousands of young lives.

"My opinion is that sex before marriage is okay as long as the couples keep to themselves, as it is the irresponsible rampant promiscuity God frowns upon. It is regarded as marriage in His eyes when two are yoked together as one and live together in love. Payment to an office of registry is not marriage in Father's eyes; marriage is the union of a couple in a sexual relationship with a loving bond for each other - not a legal bond, nor the payment of a fee. A wedding ceremony though not mandatory is enough validation."

"Children out of wedlock?"

"Lee, marriage is humankind's ceremony, not God's ceremony and the reason for wedlock was for the male to take legal possession of the female as personal property and to have children with her which then belonged to him, and no-one else was to have her.

"Although our Father validates marriage between man and woman and He sees this as a holy union to be taken with the solemn dignity it deserves, the children that are born out of wedlock are loved in his eyes just as much as those born in wedlock.

"And the ones who are not christened are cherished just as much as those who are christened, as this is humankind's ceremony, not God's ceremony." (Adam and Eve were not married, nor were Joseph and Mary when Mary conceived Jesus through the Holy Spirit.)

Chapter 7. House of Principalities

"Lee, it is Father! Let me tell all now that children born out of wedlock are my children, not theirs; and all have equal status in my house and my heart!"

"Thank you father, I think most people will see your wisdom here."

"Vehuel, what is the difference between a baptism and a christening?"

"Lee, baptism is to give the recipient acceptance into the Christian faith and is a holy ceremony signifying purification of the soul and spiritual rebirth whereas christening is the giving of a Christian name to a child and usually includes baptism."

"This Christian name will be called on the Day of Judgment if that person is still living then."

"Are either of these religious ceremonies necessary, Vehuel?"

"No Lee, they are to provide spiritual comfort for the people involved and that is all. A small Christian ceremony over a person or a child pleases Father but has no bearing whether that person enters the kingdom of heaven or not, and to think it does so is not true."

God says, "All souls are given a name when I create them and that is the name I know them by. That is the name on their personal records and that is the name they will remember when they return home. And all of their lives lived on earth will have different names. All have but one name and that is the name I have given them."

"Yahweh, then why is a living person going to be called by the name their parents gave him or her on the Day of Judgment, instead of the name you gave them when you created them?"

"Lee, it is the name of the soul entering into the spirit world. And the soul is to join the higher-self and the higher-self has the name I gave it at the time I created it."

"Thank you for clarifying that, Yahweh."

Chapter 7. House of Principalities

"Vehuel, what do you do in your spare time?"

"Lee, my time is divided into many sections and to be efficient I divide it into blocks so that the time I give to each of the church leaders is in proportion to the time I give each of the world leaders. The time I give guarding over people in my time frame is also proportional to the time I spend as a messenger."

"Thank you for your valuable input Vehuel, goodbye for now."

"Lee, goodbye and you are thinking that religion mixed with politics is a dangerous minefield to walk over!"

"Yes I was thinking that Vehuel, and it is a minefield as everybody has their own ideas on these matters; so we'll leave it there for now, and catch up again soon; goodbye."

"Lee, thank you for giving me this opportunity to speak to you about my duties today; goodbye for now my friend."

DANIEL - looks after those born 28th November to 2nd December.

"Lee, it is the angel Daniel."

"Are you Daniel, an angel from the House of Principalities?"

"Yes Lee, I am."

"Daniel, I'd like to ask you a few questions if I may, about the work you do and about your leisure time."

"My duties are divided between counseling the world leaders at their conferences and speaking to the church leaders about their policies."

"How do you speak to them, Daniel?"

"I impress my thoughts upon their minds."

"Would you like to elaborate on your duties for us please, Daniel?"

"Lee, whenever they meet to have peace talks I am there to try to keep the talks going until they agree on common ground, and I keep

Chapter 7. House of Principalities

them thinking about the task at hand instead of their own egos. I think that without our interventions there would be full-scale wars going on all over the world, as the temperament of human beings is warlike.

"It is not only the attitude, but also the vindictive responses given by some to show they are not worried what type of weapons the larger nations have. They play with the lives of millions and the power they have is enormous as your life depends on the rationality they display. And this is why we intervene to keep them from making aggressive gestures and saying too many unfriendly and stupid remarks.

"I would like to add a few words about the church leaders too as I do listen to them and give them information. I will tell you that I give them plenty of encouragement to help the people and not to keep the church funds for capital improvements, but rather to help those in need with food and clothing. And these church leaders, being of a far higher caliber than the politicians, have the needs of the people at heart and this rubs off all the way to church congregations around the world."

"What do you do after your work is done for the day, Daniel?"

"I take time to reflect on my day's work and wonder if I could have done anything more for anyone. I often feel that my work could have been better by being more efficient with my time and I often think that if I only had just spent an extra minute here or an extra minute there it would have made such a big difference.

"I keep my leisure time to a minimum and rarely have any, though this is a pleasure to take the time to speak to you and I don't mind at all, as you are doing a great service for us and your fellow human beings by telling them about us. And this will bring them to a better understanding of us and let them know that we are really here for them."

"I agree entirely Daniel; people will feel much safer and feel much better knowing that there are so many guardian angels here to watch

Chapter 7. House of Principalities

over them and to protect them, if they ask for it. Thank you for your contribution, goodbye for now."

"Goodbye, Lee, and I will look forward to hearing from you again soon."

HAHASIAH - looks after those born on 3rd December to 7th December.

"Hahasiah, are you able to speak to me for a little while?"

"Is it Lee, the messenger appointed to interview me?"

"Yes Hahasiah, are you an angel from the House of Principalities?"

"Lee, I am and I must say that it is good to finally meet you as I have been waiting for this time to come, and now you are here."

"Thank you Hahasiah. It takes a long time to interview all of you and I've been at it constantly for well over a week now. I'm feeling better and I've completed quite a number of interviews in this time. Can you tell me what you do with your time and some of the things you do?"

"Lee, my pleasure; I am always working, never resting!"

"You sound very productive then Hahasiah, is your work involved with religion and politics like Vehuel's and Daniel's?"

"Lee, my work is involved with the religions and I encourage the ordinary people to go to church. I try to get them out of their homes and into the churches so that they have a nice friendly gathering to attend.

"It is usually a very good atmosphere in church and I want them to know that Father and I listen to the sermons, and I try to think of ways that I can elaborate on the sermons so they will be inspiring and interesting.

"After greetings and introductions we sing a few hymns and we listen to the sermon, then after that we have Holy Communion; then we have

Chapter 7. House of Principalities

an offering putting money in the plate, then we sing another hymn and say another prayer.

"Sometimes we have an organ playing to sing along to and we pray and sometimes chant a canticle or two. We do all sorts of things to keep everyone interested! My life is dedicated to helping people go to church and I implant my thoughts into their hearts and their minds if they are genuine, to help them see the light, and they do!

"My work also involves the needy and those who are unable to attend for any amount of reasons, so I remind them to listen to the radio and tune into sermons that I feel will be uplifting and good for their soul. Father is pleased and loves them to take an interest in his works, too."

"What do you do in your spare time, Hahasiah?"

"Lee, my spare time is taken up going to church charities to oversee the distributions. I get the bursars to make an account of any money they have spare to provide food parcels and food vouchers for those going without. We make those without feel loved and we make them feel important enough to be thought of and help them in other matters too."

"Well thank you for doing this work Hahasiah; it's good to see that you care about all these unfortunate people in need! Goodbye for now."

"Lee, we all care for the down and out, not only me but every single one of us here cares deeply for them as life is meant to be for living, not for begging.

"And it is sad that some people have to be asking for handouts to live and it should not happen, but it does due to fallible human systems, though this will change very soon under God's system!

"We all go to great lengths to see that people have a good life but sadly we are unable to help every single person, although we try to do our best! Goodbye for now Lee and thank you."

"Goodbye Hahasiah, keep up the good work!"

Chapter 7. House of Principalities

IMAMIAH - looks after those born on 8th December to 12th December.

"Hello Imamiah, may I speak to you if you have a few minutes to spare?"

"Lee, it is Imamiah; I am very pleased to hear from you!"

"Are you Imamiah, an angel from the House of Principalities?"

"Yes I am, and thank you for asking me to make a contribution to your work. I am more than happy to provide you with as much information as you need, and more."

"Thanks Imamiah, would you like to give the readers a brief description of the duties you carry out and some of your private pastime activities?"

"Yes, by all means. My duties are to help those people looking for assistance in moral and welfare issues. I support them through the crises that face them and I help relieve them of their worries. The people looking for welfare are directed to a church or a charity and those looking for moral support are guided to seek help and advice from a knowledgeable person who can help and advise them."

"These are the duties you normally carry out as a guardian angel, but what do you do when you are not doing this sort of work, Imamiah?"

"Lee, my other duties are to distribute the words of our Father to all who will listen. I go about the world daily, visiting the smaller churches, providing them with the presence of a holy being which they feel when they are praying. That presence is sometimes me, if not Father, as I am there to do this.

"I sense that some are really in church to worship and others are there to accompany their parents. I feel their emotions as I can read into them. Some are there for the friendship and still others are there only because their neighbors are."

Chapter 7. House of Principalities

"Do you visit all denominations and all houses of worship regardless of whether or not they are Christian establishments, Imamiah?"

"No, my duties only include those places of worship that acknowledge the Son, and our Father will not visit any place that does not accept His Son!"

"Oh! Okay, then what about the religions that believe in our Father but not the Son. Do these people go to the light and will they be accepted into the Kingdom of God on the Day of Judgment?"

"All will be judged on their merits and placed at the level of spiritual awareness in the light that they have attained at the time of judgment. Only those that believe Jesus Christ is the Son of God and died for them, have been forgiven of their sins and have reached level six in the kingdom of heaven will enter the God plane in the Kingdom of God on the Day of Judgment, as Jesus Christ holds the key.

"This is the way and this is fair to those who have been true to Father, and this is fair to those who believe in the Father and the Son. And this is fair to the rest of you who want to reach a higher level of spiritual awareness, whereas those who do not shall not share in all the rewards that Father is going to provide for his flock."

"This seems to be reasonable Imamiah, now can you tell me what you do in your own time?"

"My spare time is taken up by listening to the sermons. I record these for the Book of Life which is not a book on anybody in particular, but the book includes a record of the sermons and Father thoroughly enjoys reading these as it is His pastime to do so."

"Thank you for these insights Imamiah, I feel you have provided me with more than enough and it has been a pleasure to see you again; goodbye for now my friend."

"Lee, before I go can I make a suggestion?"

Chapter 7. House of Principalities

"Perhaps you could write a book about each of us, as we have much more to tell you and we would like to be able to give you our own story if you are interested?"

"Okay Imamiah, if time allows I'll consider it. Thank you for the offer, goodbye."

"Goodbye Lee. We can tell you how long we have watched over the earth, how old we are and a lot of other personal details too; goodbye for now!"

NANAEL- looks after those, born on 13th December to 16th December.

"Hello Nanael, do you have a spare moment or two to speak to me?"

"Lee, yes by all means and please tell the people how I pronounce my name."

"Okay Nanael, I will tell them your name is pronounced as
Nan-ay-ell."

"Nanael, are you an angel from the House of Principalities?"

"Lee, yes it is me, your friend, and I am the angel who provides all of you with love and kindness and I provide this in abundance to all who seek to share in it, as it is a gift from Father to have. And I distribute it between the people and all who are able to accept it do, though some reject it."

"Nanael, I thought love and kindness came from within and was in everybody's heart, not just a gift bestowed on us whenever we needed to give it to others."

"Lee, it is in all of you but I have to bring it to the surface by putting the idea into the minds of the people otherwise it would barely see the light of day, and this gift is to be shown as much as possible, to override the emotions which tend to bring negativity to us."

Chapter 7. House of Principalities

"Are you solely responsible for distributing this love and kindness to all of humanity, Nanael?"

"I am, Lee. My helpers distribute it and I get help from the angels in other houses to do this with me and I delegate it out among those who wish to help. We all put in toward making it a much kinder and caring community and we endeavor to help the people love each other and show compassion. We especially try to impress this on the world leaders, as they are not interested in the people, just the economy and the trade that goes on and the politics of running the country. And they need to be made aware of this gift."

"This appears to be an admirable role that you have Nanael. What do you do in your free time?"

"My free time? Lee, I go to the other houses to see what they are doing there. I visit my friends in the other realms and I visit places that I have not seen before as the universe is vast and to see it is a wonderful experience beyond measure."

"Thank you Nanael, goodbye for now."

"Lee, I can tell you more if you wish! My other duties are to go to all the houses of angels and distribute goodwill and friendship too."

"Between the houses, Nanael? Do you also distribute goodwill to all people on earth?"

"No Lee, another angel is responsible for this; an archangel. I remind the angels about the gifts that they have to give out and I give them my best as I have a lot to give, and they appreciate me doing this for them."

"Thank you for sharing this with us Nanael, I will leave it there for now; goodbye, I will speak to you again soon."

"Lee, I wanted to ask you if you would be able to write a book for us, as we have all decided to ask you to write about us. We would love you

Chapter 7. House of Principalities

to tell the people about our lives without our roles or duties or hobbies and just describe the things we do and not categorize them."

"I'll certainly consider it Nanael. This would have to be a single book though that would include just one story from each of you; otherwise, I simply wouldn't have time to do it."

"Lee, I will speak to you as soon as you are free, as I want to tell you a few things in private; goodbye for now."

"Okay Nanael, goodbye."

NITHAEL- looks after those born on 17th December to 21st December.

"Hello Nithael, do you have a few minutes free to speak to me?"

"Hello Lee, I have been waiting to speak to you all morning and I see you have been adding some punctuation to our words; have you finished this?"

"Yes Nithael, are you from the House of Principalities?"

"I am and I have been in the House of Principalities for thousands upon thousands of years and I have seen everything that has passed and I have been everywhere that is possible for me to go. And I have heard all of the words in the English language and have spoken all of those words too."

"That's good to know Nithael, as you will probably have a lot of very interesting things to say and a lot of information to impart to us then."

"Lee, my duties are to oversee the people in the world's leadership roles and take a note of their integrity and this is presented to our Father daily so He can take measures to implement their decisions or to counteract them if they are amenable to this.

"Father has the power to change these decisions if they listen to Him, and He has to decide on the course of action to take as many decisions

Chapter 7. House of Principalities

are long term and many are short term; so they have long term or short term effects. Therefore, if all is balanced it becomes a very good decision, but if it is not balanced it creates a problem that rebounds and this is what Father is trying to avoid, just wanting all who live on earth to enjoy life.

"This is the main purpose, to enjoy all that is provided and it is the main reason Father provides so many wonderful things in abundance."

"This work would take you on a daily tour of the world, Nithael, and to get an idea of what all the leaders are considering doing would be a big bag full of tricky little surprises, as they all have differing opinions, views; values, moral standards and ethics too."

"Lee, it is a long trip for me and I collect and gather knowledge of the world's affairs that I need to take back to the house and impart it to all there as they want to be warned in advance of the pending changes and dangers that are coming.

"The Angel of Change implements these according to his abilities and the Angel of Good watches to make it work properly. The Angel of Prosperity watches over it all to make it worthwhile and the Angel of Industry also helps to ensure that all is carried out with efficiency. The Angel of Light is watching to bless all that transpires and many, many angels are involved in trying to ensure humans are happy.

"This brings a great sense of satisfaction and achievement to all of the angels involved. They carefully look over their handy-work later on and congratulate each other on their efforts. They then go home to wait until our Father has given His approval on the completion of their various missions, and then they are all up and running once more, to start on their next assignment."

"Thanks Nithael, now would you like share a little about your spare time activities with us?"

Chapter 7. House of Principalities

"Yes Lee, I was just going to tell you about my activities and they involve visiting the elderly in their homes, and I watch over them in their reclining chairs. Some are watching the television and some are knitting for their great-grandchildren, whereas others are listening to the radio and placing bets on the football or on the horses.

"Yet others are painting their homes and some are planting the next flower bulbs ready for the springtime. I watch all with interest as I see what they have in mind and if it is pure I bless them, and I feel as though my daily work is truly worthwhile, and the sense of personal achievement and the satisfaction I get from this work is enormous."

"Your life sounds rich and rewarding Nithael. I can only hope that one day I may have such a worthwhile life. Thank you for coming here and I'll see you again shortly; goodbye."

"Goodbye Lee, it has been a pleasure speaking to you."

MEBAHIAH - looks after those born on 22nd December to 26th December.

"Mebahiah, may I speak to you and ask you about the life you lead in the spiritual realms?"

"Hello Lee, I am pleased to speak to you again after the last time and I was wondering if you would give Golaiah a message for me as she has not contacted us, and we want her to."

"Are you the angel Mebahiah from the House of Principalities?"

"Yes Lee, that is me, and I am really happy to be here today supplying you with this information and also giving you a message to pass on to Golaiah for me."

"What is this message, Mebahiah?"

Chapter 7. House of Principalities

"Lee, I would ask her to make contact with us as we need to know what her ideas are about a number of issues, as she has not responded to any of our questions so far!"

"Mebahiah, all in good time. Even though Judgment Day is around the corner, Golaiah has some tests to pass first and will contact you and tell you what she has in mind well before then, so don't worry."

"Lee, it is about the Day of Judgment, as we have waited patiently for this and now it is in sight we are all getting very nervous, as we will need her here to guide us and direct us."

"Mebahiah, Golaiah will contact you soon, after she has first resolved some personal issues and has passed some more of Father's tests. I am sure that everything will be taken care of as Father has been working out the procedures to follow for a very long time now and He will ensure all goes according to His plans."

"Very well then Lee, we will wait patiently and now I will tell you some of the things I do as I go about my daily duties. My main role is to be the guardian angel of my leader Golaiah, who is [if she passes all of her tests] a messenger on earth and she is one of the many I look after.

"My duties are to give those in need of guidance instructions on how to go about resolving the problems at hand, and they usually follow these instructions. I hint at what they are to do to steer them in the right direction and this is the way I help. I also give them the incentive and encouragement as well as guidance and direction; and they pick up on these feelings so well it is as though I am doing it myself."

"How do you do this, Mebahiah?"

"Lee, I impress upon their minds the issues at hand and I use my problem solving skills to manipulate the situation to best suit the purposes of each individual, so from that they can then arrive at a satisfactory and conclusive resolution."

Chapter 7. House of Principalities

"In other words, you impress upon them a very clear picture of what is going on so that they can take the most appropriate action."

"Only if they ask for guidance Lee, as I have only two hands and though we do many tasks at once, the world has many and we are few."

"Well it's certainly reassuring to know that you are helping us out here, Mebahiah."

"Lee, some people need more help than others as the lack of education can be a hindrance to them because they have not learnt to exercise their minds properly. This is unfortunate as they need to be told what to do and only go on what they see and hear on television; so they are easily led and even more easily misled."

"Yes, I can understand that Mebahiah; a well rounded education is important, stimulating the mind which gives the educated a leading edge over the others, enabling them to sort out the chaff from the straw."

"Lee, also some of my time is taken up by being in places where the homeless and needy are housed and they call these places 'refuges.' I give them comfort and try to help them if possible, but some refuse to be helped which is sad as they do not listen to reason."

"Mebahiah, you can only do so much and it's really up to the people themselves, as individuals; but if they're not really capable of making groundbreaking decisions for themselves, I'm glad you're here to at least subtly direct, guide and advise them."

"Lee, I try to and I do help most of them; and the ones who do not listen eventually get helped, but it takes much, much longer."

"Thank you for this insight Mebahiah, it's good to speak to you again; take care and goodbye, for now."

"Lee, I will be pleased to help you anytime you need me and I will be helping those close to you too, if they need any help."

"Thank you, Mebahiah; goodbye."

Chapter 7. House of Principalities

POYEL - looks after those born on 27th December to 31st December.

"Hello Poyel, it is Lee; I would like to speak to you. Do you have time to tell me about your duties and anything else you'd like to offer, such as what you do when you get some free time to yourself?"

"Hello Lee! I would be glad to give you the information you want and I will give you as much as you like about my duties and my free time."

"Thanks Poyel, are you an angel from the House of Principalities?"

"Yes Lee, and I have a lot to tell you if you have time to listen. I can do many things. I do many things by myself without the others as I prefer to work independently without help. I do this so that I can be where I have to be, without being held up and I go wherever I want to go immediately. I want to help people all over the world and I do, and this is why I choose to work by myself."

"Poyel, you're a self starter, and this has many advantages if you can work independently from the others efficiently, without any holdups; do you always work alone?"

"No Lee, at scenes of major disasters we all go together to assist if possible and we can be there instantly too, as we have this ability."

"We can be on one side of the world at one moment, then on the other side of the world the next, traveling as fast as thought."

"What sort of work do you carry out, Poyel?"

"Lee, my duties are to give the faithful a serve of my wisdom and give them insights into confidential matters that others can only guess at, and the insights are about policies made by government departments. They are told the truth as to the agenda and they are able to see clearly what the issues are.

"I guide them in the decision making that is necessary to improve on these matters and I also want to impress upon you the reality of these

Chapter 7. House of Principalities

issues. And some happened last week, some are happening now and some of them will happen tomorrow.

"My other duties are to get help for those who need it and I strive to do as much as I can for them, and I help them when they are in risky situations such as traveling alone at night by train, so I keep watch over them. I keep the people inside their houses whenever the winds and hailstorms are going to break windows, and keep them inside if lightning is flashing, so they are kept out of the elements.

"The rains can lash down then as all the ones I look after will have gone to bed and have gone to sleep, after I have advised them to. And that is a good way to get some rest as it is no good staying up to listen, as the storm does not listen to you, so why listen to it?"

"Good philosophy Poyel, if the people get a good night's sleep they will wake up refreshed too!"

"My great love is to be the one giving them their new found ideas on helping others out too, as it is inspirational to do this to people, then see them going into action implementing these ideas that are really ideas from both myself and Father.

"My best idea was to make the leaders aware of the climate change which has been neglected, and the ozone layer has been overlooked too; so this will be looked at again soon, as it is not improving at all yet.

"The other great love I have is to provide insights into problem areas of poverty which lead the appropriate government officials into making vast amounts of money free to these nations which are impoverished by drought and famine, as well.

"The people receiving this relief are thankful and I personally watch this as to me it makes my work worthwhile, as they are alive through my efforts; and it is wonderful to see them thriving in the midst of these hardships, which come and go."

Chapter 7. House of Principalities

"I ensure that the officials implement these policies, giving these key people a sense of responsibility and a sense of security in their own wellbeing by making sure they are well fed and clothed without the worry of personal financial burdens weighing them down; so in that respect the plight of others is highlighted to them by direct comparison to others.

"Poyel, I see you give a lot of yourself to this end, and targeting politicians to make these donations is best as the money then comes from the public purse, not from individual people.

"Lee, my life is one of giving and I find giving is inspirational, as the majority of people are very selfish and do not have it in their hearts to give or to help others if they can get out of it. If I can, I impress the idea into their minds to help others by giving. They then find this newfound practice brings about a sense of pride, in that it can overcome their compulsive need to accumulate personal property for themselves.

"It is a rare individual indeed who is willing to part with what they perceive to be their own property, but in fact no-one owns anything at all as Father is the owner.

"And when they die they will have the same as what they were born with, leaving all worldly goods behind. Then they will see the goods and chattels that they hoarded and coveted distributed willy-nilly, and they will see that nothing was worth keeping unless it was necessary to have to live. And all other possessions are really just a clutter in their lives.

"They will then realize that to live simply is to be holy and those with many clothes and many belongings are less holy than those without."

"Thank you for your comments and your contribution, Poyel; I'd like to hear from you again soon."

"Lee, I will tell you some stories later about some well known identities and you will be amazed! Goodbye and God bless!"

"Okay, thank you Poyel; goodbye."

House of Archangels

Guardian angels residing in this house look after those born
- 1st January to 9th February -

God says, "This is my house of messengers. The archangels all reside within its walls and all the guardian angels and all the helpers within are part of the team. I look into this house more often than any other house as my team is here. I rely on them much more than the others and this is the place where I go to see if my angels are free to do my bidding, and I do the assigning of duties through this house."

NEMAMIAH - looks after those born on 1st January to 5th January.

"Lee, it is Nemamiah!"
"Hello Nemamiah, are you an angel from the House of Archangels?"
"Yes I am and I am the angel who takes the other angels to task if they are late or they do not listen to me, and I take the others to task for being lackadaisical. I take them to task for other minor things too. I discipline them and my duties are to keep them on their toes.

"I admonish them if they are not punctual and I love to give praise if they are punctual! I am the Angel of Time and I am the angel who makes the time for the rituals we carry out and I make the time for everything. And this is my main duty which keeps me fully occupied... and what else is there?"

"Do you do any work on earth helping out humanity in any way as a guardian angel, Nemamiah?"

Chapter 8. House of Archangels

"Yes of course I do and my work is to ensure that none are late for work if they ask me to get them there on time.

"And if they pray to be at a place in time to see another, I arrange it for them to arrive on time. They pray for me to help them with the timetables they look at and I help people to understand them and I tell them to catch a train or a bus depending on the time they have. It sometimes works out very well and at other times, it just works out.

"My duties entail being the Timekeeper and it is a very important job, keeping time. I am the angel who makes the events of the day all fall into place and happen in sequence, and this is why."

"Is there anything in your private life that you would like to tell me about Nemamiah?"

"Lee, my own personal time is used to entertain the angels here as I am a very good actor and my joy is to parade about impersonating them, making light of their antics, bringing all to laughter at my imitations of them. I also do some singing and if I may say so, am rather popular because of my talents in the field of entertainment."

"Thank you Nemamiah, and I'll say goodbye for now."

"Goodbye Lee, it has been nice to meet you."

YEIALEL - looks after those born on 6th January to 10th January.

"Hello Yeialel."

"Lee, it is Yeialel!"

"Are you Yeialel, from the House of Archangels?"

"Yes it is, Lee and I must say how happy I am to meet you. And this is the first meeting, so please take as long as you like to speak to me as I want to tell you as much as you need for your project, and I want to keep your details too."

Chapter 8. House of Archangels

"Thanks Yeialel, I appreciate the friendship you are all displaying toward me and the willingness you have to share a little of your private lives with us here."

"Lee, it is a pleasure to tell you about our many roles in heaven and we are delighted at the prospect of the book. We are waiting to see the expressions on the faces of all who read as we will watch everyone reading it. We will laugh to see how they look, and how they think; and how they feel, and this will provide us with a new entertainment as we have been watching some of them for most of their lives. And the ones we guard have thought many thoughts and said many things, but nothing unusual. They have not had the time to relate to any inspirational events lately, so this will give their minds a new dimension to explore, and we are looking forward to seeing how they react to it."

"Good idea Yeialel, I'm sure it will be an interesting little adventure for all of you."

"Lee, we do not go about listening in deliberately, but we will this time and this will be a way to determine if people appreciate us or not. We will be able to tell if our work is seen to be helping and if we see this it will make us very happy, and we will feel very pleased."

"Good! Though I think that you'll be a little surprised at some of the mixed reactions you get, Yeialel."

"Lee, my role is to be able to accommodate the people who have nowhere to live and I give these people a home if possible. I have been keeping people housed all the time and this is a big job too, as these people have either lost all in war, fire; flood, earthquake; tsunami or other disaster and have been unable to earn enough money to provide themselves with suitable quarters, so I help them."

"So where do you mainly work, Yeialel?"

Chapter 8. House of Archangels

"My travels are far and wide but mainly centered in South East Asia, the Pacific Basin and surrounding countries at the moment."

"I would have thought that there were still major accommodation problems in the Middle East and Afghanistan too, Yeialel."

"Lee, there are problems worldwide and the people have been resilient and I am proud to see how they rally under extreme hardship as they try to live in unbearable conditions."

"Yeialel, the people need sound government policies that will create education and employment for them as well as a strong economy to allow them to rebuild their lives."

"I agree Lee, and we strive to do this against all odds as we have no set policy of making the people change their minds. All have free will and we are not to intervene in these matters. We provide information to those who ask for it and help out groups of people or single individuals who ask God to help them."

"What else would you like to speak about, Yeialel?"

"Lee, it is nice to chat and I feel like chatting, do you mind?"

"Not at all, Yeialel, as this will give me a further insight into your life and personality and also give me a chance to get to know you better. The opportunity may not arise again for the readers either, so please feel free to say whatever you feel like saying, or whatever you think we need to hear or know."

"Thank you, Lee. I am very pleased to be here with you to tell you about the plans for your future. The future in store for all of you once the Day of Judgment has passed is to be living and working in harmony without any evil people among you.

"The life you are to enjoy will be due to an awareness of the things you need to study and learn and you will have as much time to do this in as you want. Then your planet will thrive and the people living on it will

Chapter 8. House of Archangels

make it incredibly beautiful as all will want to help in achieving this, and you will all be working toward the most beautiful place to live in that is possible to imagine.

"Your food will be in abundance as no-one will be making a profit and no-one will be trying to make money out of the other as all will share without greed and without the ways of the wicked. All will treat each other with love and respect, and then we will have a world full of good without evil, and no evil will be seen.

"Governments will not be required as the people will make their own decisions and will be far better off. The people will have meetings to decide on the best ways to provide for themselves. The people will give up the old ways and never ever go back to the ways of the world as we know it now." [17]

"It sounds very promising Yeialel, just like one big happy family."

"Believe it Lee, as it will come to pass and we know this!" [18]

"What's going to happen to the countries that will only have the meek who will inherit the earth left to run them after all the wars and disasters? These countries will be so diminished in population that just to move from one place to another will almost be impossible.

"Cars will be left everywhere with no-one to run the traffic and no-one to take care of the essential services such as the gas supplies, electricity supplies; water supplies, fuel supplies; telephones, ambulances and other essential services, too numerous to bring to mind."

"This has all been considered Lee, and special key people will be in place to administer these services and all will be well taken care of. So do not worry about it as it is the least of the things that you will be

---

[17] See (Revelation 7:14-17)

[18] See (Matthew 24:14)

Chapter 8. House of Archangels

thinking about, as all will have a new future and all will have unlimited time and potential."

"Do you know if the people left alive on earth will be living in the same cities they lived in before, or will they all be congregating in one place?"

"Lee, this judgment will take place over one thousand years, so you will not be taken by surprise.[19] All people will be judged at their allocated time and hopefully the time will start near the end of this decade, but only our Father knows this date. And only deceased souls left on the earth plane will rise at the Rapture, in an empyreal body, for judgment.

"Yeialel, will the people living on earth be aware that Judgment Day is starting when it begins to take place, in the Houses of Angels?"

"Yes, the people living now will be judged at their time of death, before their ancestors, to bring the last alive to justice first; then we will judge those who were put in the grave first, last. The people will be aware that Father has arrived with the Son to judge them and they will be amazed at this as it will be in broad daylight. And they will say, 'What's this?' And they will ask, 'What's happening?' And they will cry out, 'It's the end!'"

"Well Yeialel, it will be the end for most of them, so their worst fears will be warranted and they should be worried!"

"The people will be shaking with fear Lee, and they are to be shaking too, as our Father will have no ears for their pleas, as they have not heard the pleas of their brothers and sisters that they have forsaken. And so it will be done in heaven as it is done on earth!"

"Yeialel, there will be a lot of cynical skepticism about these foretold apocalyptic events as they seem to be highly improbable and are way beyond the comprehension and understanding of most people, and way beyond the range of normal reality. Is it possible this fire and brimstone

---

[19] See (2 Peter 3:8)

Chapter 8. House of Archangels

you're telling me about is merely to intimidate the people reading this into behaving themselves, and this end will not really eventuate at all?"

"Lee, truly you are seeing the truth now and Father has told me to remind you that you are one of His messengers and that your mind is clear! [20]

"And you see all things in perspective and you are not being misled, dreaming or hallucinating!

"And the day is now, this is your reality and we are talking to you and you are hearing us!"

"Well, Yeialel, there aren't really too many other options for me to choose from that look quite as promising as this one!

"Now, would you like to tell me what you do to relax, whenever you find yourself with a spare minute or two?"

"Lee, I love to sit by the mountain streams and watch the waters flow by and I love to see the birds of the air. I listen to them with glee and I enjoy their antics. I dearly love the natural bush settings and the natural mountain spring waters and I instill this into my people that nature is a beauty of untold measure, and to stay at home watching television instead of spending time with Mother Nature seems to me to be a waste of precious time.

"This world has to be cleaned up soon as it is becoming too polluted, and people who can get outdoors to look at what is left should do so."

"Well that should be enough for the moment Yeialel and thank you for the interview. I trust that you will return to speak to me again?"

"I will! This is only the beginning as I want to give you more details later on; goodbye, Lee."

"Okay, thanks Yeialel, goodbye."

---

[20] See (2 Peter 3:1-7)

Chapter 8. House of Archangels

HARAEL -   looks after those born on 11th January to 15th January.

"Hello Harael, are you free to speak to me for five or so minutes?"

"Lee, it is Harael!"

"Are you Harael, an angel from the House of Archangels?"

"Yes Lee, what is it you want to ask about?"

"I would like to know what your daily duties are during the time you are rostered on duty and also what you do in your leisure time."

"Lee, it is my role to give the needy a lift and I do this by bringing their attention to whatever resources are available to them. It gives them the opportunity to get ahead as sometimes it provides a little boost, just enough to help them make it through a difficult time. I feel that they can be provided for better by helping them secure a decent job, and this helps, for they are nearly always looking for suitable employment.

"The world economy is slowing at the moment and we are heading into tough times. We are here to provide help for the people and Father asks us to keep them going as well as we can. In addition to this He tells us to see that the people are able to get enough to eat and if not, to get the message to parts of the world where good, compassionate people can send donations of food and clothing.

"Donors send money for the people to go to school, provide pumps to bring them water up from the boreholes and wells, provide generators for them to have electricity and provide medicine for them so that their children may live. They provide eye care and health care, immunize them against disease and provide all manner of things including some domestic appliances and agricultural machinery."

"Yes Harael, I know of many good charities and people here who sponsor the unfortunate people living in Africa and South East Asia and

Chapter 8. House of Archangels

other parts of the world and there are some wonderful charitable organizations worldwide doing marvelous works in these places too."

"Lee, they do much for the people and without them the people would die as their governments have not got the necessary facilities to help them as they are not like other nations. They are not able to oversee the massive food shortages due to lack of infrastructure and continuous internal conflicts, which creates more problems for them.

"The wealthy in these countries use cheap labor and have no regard for the starving, as the wealthy are not hungry. They forget about the starving and pretend they are not there. And if they do see them, they avoid them as undesirables who should be kept out of sight or working for them as cheap labor.

"They delude themselves that all is well and that tomorrow is another day; today's starving will be okay, and not to worry about them, as people have always found a way to fend for themselves. But in reality many die and in truth many more will die and this adversity is avoidable."

"What can be done Harael? The governments of some of these countries receive Foreign Aid from everywhere but do not distribute it to those who need it. Some countries direct it into military activities and buy weapons of war, perhaps even sending bribes and signing major trade deals with some of the foreign government officials providing the aid!"

"The corruption is rife, Lee, and it will be addressed at the end time when this will be exposed. I will be watching it as I will provide eyewitnesses and Father will decide what to do then. This is the reason we still have to provide for the poor with charities that send people directly to the places of famine and distribute directly to those in need.

"As you are aware, the local governments divert the money for arms and thankfully, these legitimate charities are on the spot to do the work, saving lives by providing food, clothing and medicine."

Chapter 8. House of Archangels

"Thanks Harael, and what do you do with any leisure time you may have?"

"It is spent looking at the world's flowers as I love them. And everywhere I go I make a journey to see the flora and the fauna of the region, as it is my interest and I enjoy this pastime, and it is my only pastime."

"Well Harael, after Judgment Day you'll have plenty of time on your hands to have as many pastimes as you like, so with that thought my friend, I'll bid you farewell."

"Lee, let me tell you how much we are all looking forward to this time and we relish the thought too, as it will be the beginning of a new way of life for all of us here and our duties will be over. It has been a pleasure to talk to you and I will be seeing you again shortly if you don't mind, as I would like to speak to you about a few other issues; goodbye until then."

"Thank you, Harael; I'll look forward to it, goodbye."

MITZRAEL - looks after those born on 16th January to 20th January.

"Hello Mitzrael, are you free for a moment as I'd like to speak to you?"

"Lee, it is Mitzrael, and I am here now and I can speak to you for the rest of the day if you like, as my duties are over for now and my next assignment starts tomorrow"

"Are you Mitzrael from the House of Archangels?"

"I am, and I am the Angel of Health and Vitality!"

"Angel of Health and Vitality, Mitzrael?"

"Lee, you heard me properly; yes I am that angel and I go about the industrialized world seeing that people go to the gym and they are not sitting down all day as they will have heart attacks if they do. I see to it

Chapter 8. House of Archangels

that those I watch over are able to get plenty of fresh air and sunshine as the body requires plenty of movement to keep it healthy.

"The blood cells need oxygen and the brain needs plenty of oxygen to provide the body with good reflexes and to overcome tiredness. The body must have the rest it needs to rejuvenate and must have at least the daily requirement of vitamins and minerals to keep it in good physical condition, to help cope with the stresses of the day."

"That all makes good sense, Mitzrael. Do you actively encourage people to go out and exercise and eat sensibly by implanting these ideas directly into their minds?"

"Yes Lee, I encourage as many as will listen to walk for at least twenty minutes every day to stimulate their circulation; not only my own personal flock that I oversee but everybody I see, as a healthy body improves their quality of life in every way."

"Are there any other activities you do besides encouraging people to keep fit and healthy, Mitzrael?"

"Yes, I also watch their diets to see that they are not eating too many fatty foods all at once and I keep their minds fully informed about this at a subconscious level. I also watch their eating habits to see how much they need to eat to make them feel satisfied, as otherwise some of them would eat far too much without my discreet intervention."

"The amount of obese people dying of heart attacks is decreasing here lately so you must be doing a very good job, Mitzrael."

"Lee, the amount of people who disregard their food intake has to be seen to be believed as they constantly eat from little snack packs and containers. They buy take-away food as though they were not having any meals at home; and some drink far too many cans or bottles of liquid that are mostly sugars and will eventually lead to health problems. Some people smoke cigarettes that will cause health problems too and the

Chapter 8. House of Archangels

combination of these take-away snack foods, drinks and cigarettes will reduce life by many years."

"Your work must add years of life to many people then Mitzrael, which is good, as a long and healthy life is usually a productive one."

"Yes Lee, it adds about fifteen years to the life of an average individual and my contribution makes it worthwhile as I reap the benefits by directly seeing the results of my efforts."

"Well, that does make a big difference then!"

"Lee, the amount of life experience lost in the world due to the deaths of the learned, slows progress down considerably. These people are under stress and pressure and these are the ones who are less able to get about in the fresh air as they are desk-bound and not able to give sufficient time to their own physical state of wellbeing.

"My work is involved with people who are in sedentary jobs to impress upon them the importance of taking time out for their own wellbeing, rather than for the wellbeing of others, who they constantly strive to help.

"A balance is sought so that they are able to live in the world for as long as they are able to, giving of their knowledge to the world, and they are usually the ones who strive for the betterment of humankind."

"That's good of you Mitzrael; and what do you do in your spare time?"

"Lee, my spare time is spent at the beach watching the waves and I watch the boats from the beach as they go sailing by. Also, I watch the seagulls scavenging scraps from among the rocks as I love the water and am always somewhere nearby."

"Thank you for your valuable contribution, Mitzrael; it has been a pleasure meeting you."

"Lee, it has been a pleasure to meet you too and I will watch over you to see if you are eating properly!"

"Okay, thank you Mitzrael; goodbye for now."

Chapter 8. House of Archangels

UMABEL - looks after those born on 21st January to 25th January.

"Hello Umabel, are you an angel from the House of Archangels?"

"Lee, it is Umabel!"

"Thanks for responding Umabel, as I usually ask for an audience first and was trying to see if I could contact you more quickly."

"Lee, we are aware you are contacting all of us and we are ready to visit you without the normal formalities."

"Okay, thank you Umabel, do you have time to tell me a little about yourself now?"

"Yes of course, and it is my pleasure to meet you and to tell all of you about myself and also about my Father's house and the angels in heaven. My duties are my life and my life is involved in the people's happiness on earth. I love to help people, especially those who would not expect it and I do this for the reason that they are to be shown that all people are equal in Father's eyes, as He made them all."

"That's exemplary of you, Umabel. What sort of help do you provide for the people you select or are able to help?"

"I give them encouragement to approach others who hold key positions and I give them the courage to ask these people for the role or position that they have vacant. I give the people the courage to speak up for themselves if they are in court falsely accused and I give them the strength to proclaim their innocence, and they do!"

"Yes Umabel, it would be an intimidating experience to be in court with everybody there for the sole purpose of prosecuting you and putting you behind bars unless you had the ability to speak up for yourself, especially for the average person who cannot afford expensive legal representation."

Chapter 8. House of Archangels

"Lee, it happens constantly and that is why we are not happy with the death penalty as many innocent people are executed in powerful nations for crimes they have not committed, and this is dreadfully wrong."

"I am sure it happens in other countries too, Umabel, not only in those powerful nations!"

"Lee, I am pointing to countries that try the defendants in court before execution, but most developing countries execute without trial and if the accused person is innocent then they simply keep executing people until the guilty party is inadvertently killed too."

"That's right, Umabel! Yes I have heard of these mass executions in many developing countries run by dictators and have seen photos of mass exhumations and skeletons."

"Umabel, the last man executed in Australia was Ronald Ryan, in February 1967. Ryan was possibly innocent of killing a prison warder when he was escaping from jail, as years later a fellow warder confessed on his deathbed to the accidental shooting of his colleague."

"Yes Lee, this man Ronald Ryan died on the gallows with indecent haste without enough time to produce the evidence that would have prolonged and eventually saved his life."

"Why wasn't the execution stopped by the angels then, Umabel; especially if the angels Asaliah and Haniel impressed upon all those involved a doubt about Ryan's guilt?"

"Lee, their words fell on deaf ears! The execution was politically motivated and satisfied the blood lust of the wicked!"

"Well, thanks for the interesting insight into your duties and the people's lack of respect for someone's life, Umabel, now can you tell me what you do in your spare time?"

"My spare time is used productively to keep the children under my wing fully occupied. I keep them busy by letting them color in picture

Chapter 8. House of Archangels

books and I give them the creativity they display in school classrooms by drawing and sketching."

"Thanks for your time, Umabel, it has been interesting talking to you; goodbye."

"Lee, goodbye and I will let you have more detailed information if you are going to write a story about each of us later."

IAHHEL -   looks after those born on 26th January to 30th January.

"Lee, it is Iahhel!"

"Hello Iahhel, are you an angel from the House of Archangels?"

"Yes, I am Iahhel, and I do many works for our Father, including going to see the people who run the federal elections and who do all of the background work behind the scenes."

"That sounds fascinating, Iahhel. I watched the last elections here on television and got to see all the inner workings first hand."

"Lee, my duties are to watch all the background workings and record them for Father to browse over, and He looks at this later when the people are in bed asleep."

"What else can you tell me about your duties Iahhel?"

"Lee, my duties take me to the places where the governments collaborate and they talk of joining forces against a common enemy and they are all talking about this enemy."

"What can you see for us if this is to escalate, Iahhel?"

"Lee, this will antagonize opposing forces and will lead to conflict."

"Is there any good coming out of this, Iahhel?"

"Lee, it will not go away as the people will want to keep the kettle on the boil! And why ask me if war leads to good when you know better?"

"Would you tell me about some of your other duties, Iahhel?"

Chapter 8. House of Archangels

"Yes, I do have some pleasant duties and they include watching over the fish and the sea creatures that Father provides for people to eat. He watches the waters to ensure they are going to survive and He makes people aware of the sea, ensuring they take more care of it and not spill their manufactured products in it, as this makes it hard for the fish and other creatures that live in it to survive."

"Yes I know Iahhel, and we have an Environment Protection Authority keeping a vigilant watch over our oceans to ensure that we do not let any exceed the limits they set, especially regarding oil spills in our waters from bilge pumps on visiting oil tankers."

"Father is pleased with this Lee, and He applauds the care that some people are now taking as it is far better now than it was a few short years ago. The environment is steadily improving in many ways in some advanced European countries, so we are feeling a lot happier to see this. And my work has helped as I put the ideas into the minds of responsible people, and they are now implementing them."

"Well that's very helpful Iahhel, as it all started to look a bit gloomy. It's good to hear that people are now starting to sit up and take notice and starting to do something positive!"

"Lee, not all is doom and gloom as the world is full of beauty. And we are here to keep it that way for as long as possible, as the people will need to have somewhere to live that is habitable; and they strive to keep their own backyards neat and tidy. The main problem facing us is the pollution from car exhausts and we are thinking about this and have decided to intervene and help with this soon."

"Well, that's the main thing Iahhel; that is, to ensure we have fresh air to breathe to keep us alive by reducing greenhouse gases, retarding the depletion of the ozone layer and slowing down global warming."

Chapter 8. House of Archangels

"Lee, we are working on many ideas at the moment to help humans keep the planet habitable. These ideas are then given to specific people to implement into their designs and they produce efficient systems to reduce energy usage and wastage, and we do this."

"Can you give me an example of one of these ideas, Iahhel?"

"The idea that is most ignored is the most useful Lee, and that is to obtain heat energy from beneath the surface of the earth and transfer it to the surface for conversion into electricity, super-sized refrigeration plants, and water purification plants."

"How do you propose we get so much heat energy to the surface from beneath the ground, Iahhel?"

"I am trying to implant the idea into the minds of those in this field to drill down to the source of heat and then transfer this heat to the surface by installing superconductors that require little or no maintenance."

"Okay, well that seems to be a good idea Iahhel; and what do you do when you find yourself with a few spare minutes?"

"Lee, I go to the seaside and watch the waves washing up onto the beach, and I look at the beautiful sand and at the horizon contrasting the ocean waters from the sky. And I watch the clouds floating by and this gives me great pleasure to see.

"Then when I have had my fill of this beauty I go into the mountains, smell the nectar of the mountain air; listen to the buzzing sounds from the little insects and watch the animals scurrying about in their habitats, frolicking in the sunshine; and this gives me immense pleasure!"

"Thank you for your contribution Iahhel, and I'm very pleased to have met you."

"Lee, I am happy too, and please feel free to contact me at any time as I have plenty of things to talk about if you want to hear some of them."

"Goodbye and thanks, Iahhel."

Chapter 8. House of Archangels

ANAEL - looks after those born on 31st January to 4th February.

"Hello Anael, may I speak to you?"

"Lee, it is Anael."

"Hello my friend, are you Anael from the House of Archangels?"

"Hello Lee, yes I am and I am really happy to hear from you, especially tonight after your hard day's work. And I really would like to say you are doing a marvelous job and I want to tell you that we are pleased with you for doing this."

"Well, thank you Anael, that's nice to know."

"Lee, it is very good to meet you and I am pleased, and we are all very excited about it.

"I have several duties and the main thing I do is to watch the house and keep the others out of here! The others are the angels from the House of Angels. They are always barging in without asking and we are tired of it as they take up the time we need to do our work.

"We allocate assignments to each of them and we discuss our workloads, watch what we accomplish and record it so then we can try to better it, as we are constantly striving to become more effective and more efficient.

"Lee, the Christian name you use is not your heavenly name and we all know you here by the name of Oanedus that Father gave you when He created you. We know that it is you from your aura and you have a frequency that you oscillate at that we can pick up.

"All people have a frequency they vibrate at though most people are hard to distinguish between, as many are on the same frequency at times and they can be mistaken, so we always address those we speak to by their name first. And we do not speak to any in spirit without asking

Chapter 8. House of Archangels

them their name first as then we have little or no doubt as to whom we are communicating with."

"Are there ways you can distinguish one spirit from another without knowing their name or which frequency they oscillate at, Anael?"

"Lee, it is difficult then and if they give us the wrong name, we find it hard as we expect them to be the spirit associated with that name. If we have any doubt we can quickly delve into their innermost thoughts to identify them and find out which level they reside on."

"Anael, you say it is not difficult to have someone impersonate another in the spiritual realms as, unless you are there to see their aura you cannot know who they are."

"Lee, yes and this is always a problem with the unclean spirits on the earth plane who are not in the light, and they will be likely to perish, so they have no compunction about telling lies."

"Lee, it is Father!

Lee, it can be hard for the angels to differentiate between the spirits residing on the earth plane as they are in the majority and all run at a frequency similar to each other. And even their auras are similar. One way we can ascertain between them is to look into them and read their minds, which is what I do to determine who they really are as they are deceptive. That is why it is important to identify any that you are speaking to whenever you summon them from this side, as they can deceive you unless you demand to know if they are from the light. They are compelled to answer this truthfully as I have made them unable to give the wrong answer. That is why it is always best to ask, 'Are you from the light?' "

"Thank you Yahweh."

Chapter 8. House of Archangels

"Lee, it is Anael. Some try to pass themselves off as other spirits and this sometimes works and we are all deceived. The main perpetrators are evil spirits from the earth plane presenting themselves as highly evolved individuals from level six, the level of higher learning and they take the opportunity to trick us and mislead us with their lies. And it is easy to do as the ones here are not into telling lies, so we have a very trusting audience and when a liar accesses our home it devastates us."

"Well that's understandable Anael, as no-one likes being lied to and you are no exception. It's fortunate they can only access you through thought communication and not enter your realm from their level, as it would create utter confusion with all these lying little demons creating havoc for you."

"Lee, we do not have them in our house and they are not able to travel there, but they can communicate with us if summoned and we often speak to one or the other who is here as we knew them on earth. Some were really nice people but then did illegal things such as supply teenagers with drugs, so they remain here on the earth plane to pay."

"Anael, what do you do in your spare time?"

"Lee, my time is taken up with making clay figurines and we love doing this. We collect the clay and then we push it and pull it and we knead it and we roll it until we think it is soft enough to use and then we shape it and fire it in the sun, and we have this for a hobby.

"My other leisure time is spent taking photos of people in my mind's eye to capture their beauty and youth so that they will have a lasting image to see when they want to review the lives they have lived."

"It sounds like a lot of fun to me, Anael. I'll catch up with you again later; thank you and goodbye for now."

"Lee, it has been nice to talk to you; and thank you too. Please keep in touch! Goodbye."

Chapter 8. House of Archangels

MEHIEL - looks after those born on 5th February to 9th February.

"Hello Mehiel, may I speak to you?"

"It is Mehiel, and yes, please stay and talk to me for as long as you like if you need the information now."

"Are you Mehiel from the House of Archangels?"

"Lee, yes and it is Mehiel, the angel who used to be a personal friend of yours when you were last in the heavenly realms, and I know you very well."

"Well that's an advantage you have over me that I don't have, Mehiel, as I can't consciously remember the times between my past-lives unless meditating and in touch with my higher-self or examining the Angelic Records."

"True, Lee, and you did many things in your previous lives that were exemplary and we are all pleased to know you, and we are all happy to see you again. We are all very pleased to be able to talk to you as we miss you here, and we want to let you know this."

"Thank you Mehiel, we must catch up soon. The reason I've called you here today is to ask you if you can tell me a few things about yourself, such as the things you do all day and whatever else you would like to volunteer about your personal life."

"Lee, the angels are all busy here due to the amount of traffic flowing in and out and also the archangels reside here, though some are always looking after the higher houses as we are in charge of them."

"Do these houses you live in have physical boundaries, and can you describe your house to me Mehiel?"

"Lee, we are in a house that does have walls, and does have floors; and does have windows, and it is similar to the houses of old where they had an external and internal courtyard, with mosaic tiled floors and

Chapter 8. House of Archangels

monumental columns. Moreover, we love the way our house is built and this is what it is like; and it is beautiful to behold and it does have physical boundaries."

"Do you walk on solid ground or just float about; and is your house built on solid ground or is it floating in the atmosphere, somehow?"

"Lee, how can a house be floating about in the air?"

"That's why I'm asking you to explain where it is to us, Mehiel, as some people seem to think the kingdom of heaven is above, in the sky; and that's why I would like you to explain it to me and to our readers."

"Lee, this dimension is as real as yours is! The houses to us are just as solid as your houses and we have to look after them as you do. They are built on the ground here and this angelic dimension is accessible to you when you become one of us after the Judgment."

"Mehiel, we have physical bodies and you don't, so how can you live in houses like this?"

"Lee, our presence is in the shape of a human though it is a very superior form. We do not have the same bodily functions that you do and we do not age nor do we have any medical problems.

"Neither do we eat or sleep as it is not necessary for us to do so, and we want to use the time to our own advantage as the world is so big and we are so small it takes all of us to keep it in harmony with the daily happenings."

"Mehiel, the spirits in the five levels of the light waiting for Judgment do not have any specific form, do they?"

"Lee, they do and they have a form of body which can be seen if they want this, but it is a form of energy and if it is seen it may appear more as a vague mist or translucent vapor. The orbs people see are the earth bound souls of those unable to access the light and the ghosts are lost souls who manifest regularly, as they are tormented."

Chapter 8. House of Archangels

"Mehiel, do the spirits in the light live in solid houses too?"

"No Lee, spirits have all the same senses you have to enjoy their wonderful surroundings except they have no physical body and they experience the same type of physical sensation that people do who lose a leg and think it is still there; it has feeling but no presence."

"Mehiel, can you describe what the earth bound souls live like?"

"Yes Lee, these souls have not progressed to the light as spirits but have free range over the earth; however they have no way of communicating except by thought and thought alone as they are deprived of all their sensory faculties.

"And they are there for one reason and one reason alone, and that is to dwell on their mistakes, and they are there waiting for the day when Father will call them to account."

"Mehiel, do earth bound souls and lost souls live in and take up the same space we live in?"

"Yes Lee, it is completely incorrect to think they live in the sky or higher than you do. They all live in the same place and space as you, and on the same ground level as you do.

"They are within reach of people all the time as they need to know where they are, and this keeps them placed as otherwise they would become totally confused and disoriented.

"This is one of the fears they go through and also explains why lost souls usually manifest as ghosts in a place that is familiar to them."

"Thanks for giving me this extra bit of information Mehiel, and apart from your duties, this helps to explain a few more things that some people may have been unaware of before."

"Now Lee, my duties entail looking after the physicians in the world who give medical prescriptions to people, and I oversee those who ask for my guidance and they receive my help."

Chapter 8. House of Archangels

"I tell them the best way to go about their work, and I advise them about their patients and give them knowledge about each of their patients, so that a ready cure may be effected."

"What are your spare time activities Mehiel?"

"Lee, I go to the places that I have heard about and I look at them and catalog them for my scrapbook. Then I look at the maps and wonder where to go next, as I like to see as much as I can, and I do these activities in my leisure time.

"Also, say to the people my life is for them and my leisure is also in reflecting on my exposure to their past-life memories. And I now look at the progress they have made in this present life and give them guidance relative to their previous needs in the immediate last life lived.

"And I give them insights into the life they have lived before, and some are directed toward the people and the living relatives they had then.

"And some know these people now but have no idea they were family from another life. And some are living within close proximity to their past-life families and some are working together in harmony too.

"Some call these friends, 'soul mates' and some are best friends and some are colleagues as it has been imprinted into their soul to relate to their past existence through the present, and vice versa.

"And those in spirit are with people who were their aunts and uncles, brothers and sisters, fathers and mothers over many lives; so the love they have for each other here is greater than the love they had for their neighbors on earth as they were bonded by flesh and blood in life and are connected to each other through many family bonds in spirit."

"Thank you Mehiel, I'll contact you again soon when the need arises, goodbye for now."

"Lee, we would all like to talk to you more often and we will from now on. Thank you too, and goodbye."

House of Angels

Guardian angels residing in this house look after those born
- 10th February to 20th March -

God says, "These angels are my special purpose team and I use their skills in conveying my plans to all who will listen. In addition they are the ones I tell my most trusted secrets to first, as they are to impart them to humanity. I tell them that they are to distribute my blessings and my words among the people. And I tell them to provide relief and comfort, and to help the people in all manner of earthly matters."

DAMABIAH - looks after those born on 10th February to 15th February.

"Damabiah, are you free to help me with my work for a few minutes?"
"Lee, it is Damabiah!"
"Hello Damabiah, are you an angel from the House of Angels?"
"Lee, it is me, Damabiah, and I am an angel of the Lord God and I carry out his work. And I do this daily and I do this nightly and I will always do this for my Father, as He is the one who loves us. He is the one who provides all things to all people and He is the one I cherish, and He is the one who cherishes me!"
"Thank you for coming here Damabiah; now, would you mind telling me about some of the duties you carry out?"
"Lee, I go to the people in need and find out what troubles them. Then I find specific data to help them with and follow it up. Also, some of them ask Father if He can provide for their friends too, and I do this. And I get the other angels to follow up their friends as these other angels have

Chapter 9. House of Angels

specific roles, and they are able to provide the specific relief that is required from them. Then the people who are saved from the dilemma they are in are left to fend for themselves in a much, much better position than they were in before they prayed to our Father to help them out."

"You have an admirable occupation, Damabiah! Your invaluable work must keep many people alive and well."

"Lee, the people who do not pray to our Father sometimes die of starvation and we weep, but Father says that they have not heard of Him in their hearts and therefore He has not heard of them."

"An interesting paradox and a tragic set of circumstances, Damabiah! All who deny Father will themselves be denied! Now tell me, what do you do in your spare time if you get any?"

"Lee, I intermingle with the down and out and see if there is a reason for their plight. Sometimes they are sad because of the way they have been treated in childhood and sometimes they are grieving for a loved one, and are hurting deeply inside. Sometimes they are simply out of employment and need to be able to find a job. And the ones who are not drunk and the ones who are not drugged are the people I try to help first, as the others need more time to turn around.

"And the angel who looks after them is hovering close by as his duties are to keep them alive and his duties superimpose on mine; and we have many other angels doing their duty who are here too."

"It's certainly good to know that so much help is at hand for us if we ask Father for it, Damabiah!"

"Yes Lee, it is and some ask for help from Jesus and some ask for help from the Virgin Mother. Still others pray to the Saints for help, though whoever they pray to, it is us responding to the call and we dispatch one of our team to see what can be done."

Chapter 9. House of Angels

"Thank you for your contribution, Damabiah, and it has been nice to meet you. Not long before starting these interviews I had only met about twenty on the team of guardian angels and now I've met nearly all seventy two of you!"

"Lee, we are glad to have you do this for us and we appreciate it, so take care of yourself and look after yourself, and do not over indulge in eating as it is not holy. I wish you all the best if I do not get to speak to you until you have finished this task; goodbye and good luck with it!"

"Goodbye Damabiah."

MANAKEL - looks after those born on 16th February to 20th February.

"Hello Manakel, are you there?"

"Lee, it is me, Manakel."

"Good! And how are you, Manakel?"

"I am well Lee, and I want to ask you a few questions, if I may?"

"Certainly, but first, are you Manakel from the House of Angels?"

"Yes it is, and I am wondering if you could tell me why you are writing this book?"

"There are several reasons, Manakel, the first reason being that I was asked to write this by Gabriel and then later, by Golaiah. Also it is to let all people know that you are here to help them if they need you, and now Yahweh has asked me to write another book for Him following on from here using this as an introduction; lastly, any income will be used to help others requiring assistance."

"Lee, is it okay to give your hard earned money away?"

"Manakel, I'm not going hungry and others are, so why shouldn't I help out if I'm able to?"

"Lee, this is good to hear and we are helping the needy too."

Chapter 9. House of Angels

"Yes I know, Manakel, and all the angels are God's workers, helping to keep the human race on its feet and helping the world cope with one major disaster following after another."

"Lee, we enjoy our work as it gives us purpose, not like the people who wander about aimlessly! We are the angels who decide on how to supply the milk and the honey to those industrious workers who work hard and how to supply the crumbs off the table to the rest!"

"Are you an angel of supply, Manakel?"

"We are the angels who transport supplies and we watch over those delivering these products as they keep the nations fed. Without food people would be unable to live and the work we do is imperative for human survival, and our work is the hardest work too!

"We go with large ship loads of cargo and watch to ensure that the crews follow safety procedures, and if they ask for our protection we are there for them and those who neglect to ask, miss out."

"What other things do you do, Manakel?"

"I personally watch over the transport of life saving blood supplies and personally escort the pharmaceuticals for the many surgical operations, to ensure they arrive safely in time for the people needing them, so the amount of work I do is staggering."

"Well that is admirable work, Manakel. What do you do when you get the chance to have a few spare minutes to yourself or have any free time?"

"I always visit the elderly and I remember when a sad and lonely old gentleman lived nearby and was always saying his prayers. One day he called on God to take him home as he wanted to die, so God in His pity sent down an angel to bring him home and I saw him and said, 'What are you doing?' and the angel said, 'I am taking Jim to his guides so that

Chapter 9. House of Angels

they can escort him to level two,' and I said, 'Jim is far more advanced than level two!'

"He turned around and said, 'Do not tell me how to look after those in my realm, as I am the Angel of Human Affairs!' and I said, 'This man is my friend, please do not take him! This man will recover soon, as the Angel of Healing is nearby and I will get him to help!'"

"What happened then, Manakel, did it end up alright?"

"He did not take him and the gentleman felt much better after we stayed with him to cheer him up, and his melancholy soon faded away."

"It sounds like it was a close call for this elderly man, Manakel; what happened to him?"

"Jim lived happily for many years after that and he said his prayers to Father every night with renewed faith. And Father reminded me of this as He was pleased that I cared enough to intervene and stop Jim from coming home before he had developed further, spiritually."

"Is there anything else you'd like to say before we finish, Manakel?"

"I would like to add a few quick comments about the way the world is heading, and it is going to be brief!"

"Tell the readers to be on the alert and not to listen to the propaganda about the Middle Eastern people in Iraq being at war with them as they are not! And tell them that the people of Afghanistan are not! The leaders of some nations are disrupting the peace, so do not keep the animosity and the hurt and the hatred pent up for the common people, as they are not involved!"

"Okay, thank you for your contribution, Manakel, goodbye for now."

"Goodbye Lee, keep up the good work. I will speak to you again shortly."

Chapter 9. House of Angels

EYAEL -   looks after those born on 21st February to 25th February.

"Hello Eyael, are you there?"

"Lee, I am here; how are you?"

"Well, like you Eyael, I have a lot going on at the moment and soon I expect to see daylight at the end of the tunnel. Then I'll be back on track, I guess."

"Lee, we are all very busy too and this is how we like to be!"

"Me too, I like to be busy to keep my mind off all the external events happening worldwide at the moment. Are you Eyael, an angel from the House of Angels?"

"I am, and I am pleased to meet you, finally, and we have been discussing you here as you are still writing about us. We want to thank you and this work will be seen by many, and our words are to be seen by many. This makes us happy as this is new to us as you know."

"Yes Eyael, I am surprised that other channelers who are able to speak to the angels have not tried to interview you too!"

"Lee, it was never proposed and we never thought of it either as we are far too busy, normally. This is the only time since I can recall that we have had free time as we now have many helpers who are doing our duties with us, and we are free to speak to you and spend more time with each individual who asks Father for help.

"Now we are able to do a better job as we can spend the time to get all of the relevant details of the problem at hand and try to address it at grass roots level. And we are striving to do this as we want all of the people to enjoy life as much as possible and not have a multitude of ongoing problems facing them daily."

"Eyael, would you mind telling the readers how you pronounce your name?"

Chapter 9. House of Angels

"Lee, this name of mine is pronounced Eye-ell and it is the name I was given by our Father."

"Thanks Eyael, as some names are not pronounced as they are spelt in the English language, most originally being from the Old Hebrew.

"Can you intervene physically in people's lives, Eyael, or is all of your work done by impressing information into their minds, making their conscience's prick them?"

"Lee, we can intervene if it is crucial to do so and we often do unbeknownst to the recipient. We do other sorts of things too, such as change the weather and this is becoming more prevalent lately as atmospherically, conditions are becoming more polluted and we have to monitor it daily now."

"That's interesting if not worrying, Eyael; now would you like to tell me a little about the duties you carry out?"

"Lee, by all means and they are the duties I prefer to do as I want to carry out the duties my Father has allocated to me happily, and they are to keep the people informed of what is happening. I tell them to read certain books and buy certain magazines and newspapers, and listen to certain radio stations. And I inform them of pending news as well if it looks imminent that it may create problems for them.

"They think this is their sixth sense and they call this intuition, but it is not intuition, Lee; it is me and my guardian angel helpers, helping me with this all over the world, and the people's spirit guides are there to help them in their daily lives too."

"Thanks Eyael, now can you tell me about your spare time activities if you have any?"

"My activities are to keep the people informed and this is all I do as I cannot see any other activity being more enjoyable than this!"

Chapter 9. House of Angels

"Do you visit the mountains or look at the scenery, or involve yourself with Mother Nature, Eyael?"

"Lee, this is part and parcel of all the things I do as the people I inform are from everywhere and I take in these sights and drink in the beauty of these sights as I visit them."

"Okay Eyael, thanks for all of the information you've provided me with; I'll bid you farewell for now."

"Thank you too, Lee. Goodbye, until we meet again!"

HABUIAH - looks after those born on 26th February to 28th February, and on 29th February of each leap year.

"Hello Habuiah, do you have time to speak to me right now?"

"Hello Lee, yes I will stop my work to speak to you as I have been waiting for this day and this is the time I thought you would be here for me, and I have made provision to have it free for you."

"Thanks Habuiah, we haven't met before so thank you for stopping work to be here; it's nice to meet you."

"Lee, the pleasure is all mine! My work is mainly involved in watching over people in palliative care and at this moment in time I am free as my helpers have arrived."

"Habuiah, just a formality, are you an angel from the House of Angels?"

"Yes Lee, and it may be only a formality, but a very important one, as some demons thrive on impersonating us, and we get annoyed with them doing this. This is why it is so important for you to ask who you are speaking to, and get them to verify who they are. Father has made it very difficult now for spirits to tell people a lie about their identity when challenged, if they are not the one in question."

Chapter 9. House of Angels

"Habuiah, I have wondered about this as no evil spirit from the spirit world seemed willing to tell me a lie about their identity when asked. Souls left on the lowest level, the earth plane, known as evil spirits are usually unscrupulous liars, so how can they be made to tell us the truth about their identity, if only challenged verbally?"

"Lee, spirits or demons cannot speak to any living soul unless they have a means to communicate and only experienced spirit mediums can manage this. The ordinary people who contact spirits by using the Ouija board do not know that they are contacting demons and are left to hear lies and sometimes believe them. Father has made a strict rule for evil spirits and demons to adhere to, and that is, if asked where they are from they are to tell the truth and if they do not they will be extinguished immediately, the same as if they had possessed somebody.

"Habuiah, if a person has lived say, sixty lives and some lives have been very good whereas other lives have been very bad, what is the criterion that determines on which level the higher-self resides; or are all these past-lives residing on different levels until Judgment Day?"

"Lee, the higher-self is your spirit that is residing at the level of awareness your soul has previously reached in the light and it is not a lot of separate souls. The soulless higher-self is your collective-unconscious with a collective memory of all your past-lives, each life having had the same soul as you have in this life now; and with the living memories you are experiencing now, your soul will go to join it at death, making you complete once more in spirit."

"The fact is that if some previous lives of a spirit have been fairly good and the very last one has not, makes it a difficult process to determine the level in the spiritual realms that this spirit will reside at."

"But it is worked out by us, the angels, at the time of death of each of these souls. Then they are escorted to whatever level they have

Chapter 9. House of Angels

attained, by their spirit guides, after we have taken them to see what they have done and have shown them their Angelic Records. From the scrolls we determine and acknowledge whether they are worthy of the level in the light they are placed at."

"Habuiah, this seems rather complex. For example, we know the Emperor Nero led a very bad life. So if in the event his family prayed to God for him to be forgiven and this was granted, that life which was only one of Nero's lives would be forgiven and his soul would then be able to rejoin his higher-self at judgment?"

"Lee, this is true and when you pray for individuals losing their way it is best to pray for their soul; so all lives associated with their higher-self are then equal enabling that conscious soul to then merge into a collective-consciousness of the higher-self, in spirit; in the light, at judgment."

"Habuiah, Father must have a reason for this; do you know what it is?"

"I do not, though this appears sensible to me; and really, those like Nero who have been very bad are not allowed to reincarnate and his soul remains on the earth plane to this day. *If* he was forgiven he may not perish at judgment, but he, then being merged with his higher-self would still be severely punished, being banished to the pit to dwell on his mistakes and would not ever be allowed to enter the light again.

"All of a soul's previous lives are separate in their own right and the individual has been led into each new life experience without prior knowledge. This is the way Father determines a soul's worthiness to enter the light and reincarnate; and reincarnation is only fair as what else would you do in the light, unless you wanted to remain in spirit forever?

"And Father wants to see the earth thrive and He wants to have living beings tend to it. That is why He created the earth, so that it could be groomed by people tending it, and this is part of His overall plan."

"Thanks Habuiah, and what is your specific role in all of this?"

Chapter 9. House of Angels

"My duties are to oversee the people who are in the throes of dying and I find that people who are dying are frightened of this beforehand, so I make them comfortable. I tell them that everything is going to be fine and they hear me very well as the connection between them and the spirit world is heightened at this time.

"They can hear me and see me and they can converse with me, and they are allowed to do this before crossing over as our Father feels it is only right to do this for them, and they leave the earth feeling a sense of peace and happiness."

"So this applies to all, even those wicked souls who have to remain in hell on the earth plane with other sinners and demons, Habuiah?"

"Lee, it does and all are treated with love and kindness at this time, and all are escorted by their spirit guides and counseled. They are all treated the same and even those remaining in hell on the earth plane have nothing to complain about as they are well looked after.

"And those left on the earth plane are left with billions of other unworthy souls to converse with and commiserate with by thought and thought alone, being deprived of all their physical senses."

"Habuiah, what do you do when you have any spare time to yourself?"

"My spare time is taken up looking after my spirit friends in need and they are the ones I help as they are the ones in my realm. They are worthy beings and these are of course my helpers, and these are the ones I spend all of my spare time with as we discuss issues and we talk about everything. And we laugh, and we cry, and we commiserate and share in the good times too."

"Thank you for your time Habuiah. The time you've spent with me today has been well worthwhile and has given us all a few more insights into the mysterious spirit world, opening it up for us just a little more. We're learning a little bit more from each one of you."

Chapter 9. House of Angels

"Lee, the world has more to it than meets the eye and the world is full of mysteries that are not yet told. The world is far more interesting than most know about and most are to be in for a surprise, for when the Day of Judgment is upon us, they will realize that this life is only a small part of their overall existence. And the worthy are to be transferred into another reality that will be wonderful for them, and they will be overjoyed at the beauty and the abundance of all things that Father is going to provide for them, in His house.

"I will say goodbye now Lee, lest you miss out on some important appointments and I will talk to you again as I enjoy your company. Today has been good for me, too."

"Goodbye Habuiah, and thank you, I'll be in touch with you again soon."

ROCHEL - looks after those born on 1st March to 5th March.

"Hello Rochel, it is Lee. Are you free to speak to me for awhile?"

"Lee? Yes I have been anticipating you wanting to speak to me. Thank you for asking me and I am very happy to meet you. Father has spoken to all of us here and told us about you and your work."

"Yahweh has spoken to you about me? Well, I presume that you will know a fair bit about me and my work then Rochel. Yahweh speaks to me for at least a couple of hours nearly every day now about the ways of the world and we know each other very well."

"As a matter of course, are you Rochel, an angel from the House of Angels?"

"Yes Lee, and my role in the house is to provide assistance to the archangels and I also provide assistance to the angels who need any, as it is important that all the duties are carried out promptly and efficiently. If

Chapter 9. House of Angels

they are not, sometimes catastrophes are left to happen when they could have been averted.

"We strive to keep the winds from blowing too hard and the waves of the seas from rising too high. We strive to keep the storms from raining down too hard and we strive to keep the snow and the hail from piling up too high. We try to iron it all out and create a balance, as the people cannot live on the planet if we do not keep it habitable.

"Therefore, Father directs us to do this work to keep it intact. And if we are somehow unable to do it, for one reason or another, such as when a catastrophe strikes, we are left feeling disappointed and we are left feeling as though we should have done more to divert it!

"The helpers you asked Father to provide us with were here none too soon as we now require more and more help to cope with the ever changing conditions on earth. This will become more difficult as time goes by although a few concerned people are now trying to take measures to fix some of it. They are now planting trees and they are now trying to keep the ships from spilling crude oil into the waters.

"And the garbage is now placed into the proper waste collection bins for recycling instead of washing into the sea, and the toxic chemicals are now stored much more safely in warehouses. The people are gradually becoming more environmentally aware as they become better educated.

"The governments are being shown by the scientists the damage that can be avoided by taking steps in the right direction now before it is too late to change, and this is why we try to keep the atmosphere and the water clean. The people are trying to keep it clean now too and some advanced environmentalists are making other people more aware, by badgering them into action. They are the ones who are looking after the planet and they are the ones who are going to be rewarded for their

Chapter 9. House of Angels

efforts, and they are the ones we love very much! They are to be exalted and our Father exalts them, and tells us so!"

"Thank you Rochel, you certainly have a few things to say and this is good to hear. Is there anything else you would like to tell me about while you're here?"

"Lee, the world is heading toward a major change soon and the world's people are going to have to get used to it as the changes are very big, and this change includes the land masses and includes the geographical co-ordinates. The people will have to make new maps and they will have to make many changes as the world is due to start shifting off its present axis. This shift will create hotter summers and colder winters, and parts of the world that are now land will be underwater and parts of the sea now unseen will be parts of the land."

"Well that does not surprise me one little bit, Rochel, as the polar caps are melting and this will cause a massive displacement of water which weighs one kilogram per liter."

"Lee, as long as the people are aware of it and they take measures to do something about it, it is possible to delay the problem but they must act now! It must be taken seriously as the earth is only able to withstand so much, and it is reaching the point where fluorocarbons, methane gases, carbon dioxide and exhaust gases from all the car and aircraft engines are creating temperature rises, and this must be seen to now!"

"Now, Rochel?"

"Yes Lee, it is very important if you want to divert it for the time being until proper measures can be put in place."

"Measures? What sort of measures, Rochel?"

"Lee, we need at least one day per week worldwide without car exhaust pollution."

"Okay, thanks for the warning Rochel, though I have no idea how to

Chapter 9. House of Angels

divert this catastrophe as no-one will take any heed, and even if they did it would probably be impossible for them to do anything about it now."

"Lee, it is bound to happen eventually and this warning is merely a formality, so be aware of the coming events and take all the necessary precautions."

"Thanks Rochel, now tell me, what do you do in your spare time?"

"Lee, I go about the planet and I look at the way it is heading and I think about the consequences of the modern industrial processes and how to minimize any damage that is caused. I report this to Father and He dispatches a team to deal with it and they disburse the atmospheric gases and replenish the oxygen to sustain life as you people are depleting it constantly. And Father fixes this all the time by providing more trees in the environment that absorb these harmful gases and replaces them with fresh oxygen."

"Rochel, why doesn't Father ask the angels to cool the atmosphere down, at least enough to stop the polar caps from melting?"

"Lee, we are cooling it down and even with our constant efforts it is a losing battle. The polar caps are still melting and to reverse it we would have to have another ice age."

"We will just have to adjust to the changes that are imminent then Rochel. People are very adaptable, so the survivors will quickly get used to the new environment when the time comes."

"Lee, it will be a time when those people left alive have to adapt to a diminished planet with a new environment and seasonal changes and they will find they can adapt; and life, though much harsher will go on."

"Well, thank you for all these interesting though alarming insights Rochel, I'll keep in touch with you, so will say goodbye for now."

"Lee, it has been good to meet you and I will keep you informed, goodbye."

Chapter 9. House of Angels

JABAMIAH - looks after those born on 6th March to 10th March.

"Hello Jabamiah, are you free for a few minutes?"

"Lee, it is Jabamiah, from the House of Angels."

"Are you from the light, Jabamiah?"

"Yes, I am from the light."

"Thank you for indulging me as I had to check you out as you're well aware. Jabamiah, may I ask you to tell me a little about yourself as you are here for an interview to provide us all with some information, aren't you?"

"Lee, I am and I will tell you that I am the angel who disturbs the workers who sleep on the job and I keep people alert, and I always try to make them concentrate on the task at hand, instead of daydreaming!"

"Well, that's a good idea, Jabamiah, I mean who would like to be flying as a passenger in an airplane if the cabin crew were half asleep or daydreaming?"

"Lee, it is my role to ensure they are awake and I look into the jobs of millions every day, and I look at their brain activity and tell them, 'Hey, it's coffee time!' or I put it into their minds to talk to someone to bring them round and keep them on the ball."

"I had no idea that angels did such diverse things as that, Jabamiah, a very sensible idea though and an honorable occupation. This probably saves countless lives and countless hours of lost productivity and is a very valuable role you play. Whoever would have thought that an angel was watching over you, to keep you awake on the job at hand?"

"Thank you Lee, as it is hard to convince some what a difficult and valued profession I have and I am very proud to do this work. And I save many people from disaster by prodding them awake, right at the crucial time they need me!"

Chapter 9. House of Angels

"What can you tell me about your spare time activities, Jabamiah?"

"Lee, I go all over the world collecting information on people's habits and I discuss these with the other angels at home. We debate on the practicalities of these habits, and we look at them and we question the value of them, and we analyze them.

"And we take turns to watch the people who have these habits and try to discover why they have them and what makes them tick. We wonder about the why's and the wherefore's and this debate rages on all the time, and every day we discover another with habits that are peculiar. We discuss it and we look, and we look again and we wonder, and sometimes we are left speechless! And at other times we are left looking in absolute amazement at these habits!

"Some are good habits and some are bad habits and some are useless habits and some are obsessive habits and some are compulsive habits. We examine them all in minute detail, the ins and the outs of them and looking into these habits has become an extensive pastime for me and my friends, who pursue it."

"Well Jabamiah, your pastime seems just as unusual as watching out for people who jeopardize lives by dozing off! You certainly lead a busy life and I'm sure that you must be kept fully occupied with many tired, worn out people with strange habits to watch over all day."

"Lee, I am always very busy and I am always looking for other things to do as well if I can find time to fit them all in. And if someone is in need of assistance and I am close-by, I drop everything and rush over to see if I can do anything, and then I do whatever I can to help."

"That is probably why you're on the team as a guardian angel then, Jabamiah, as you seem more than willing to help people in trouble."

Chapter 9. House of Angels

"Yes, I know, Lee, and I feel I do a very, very good job of it too. And if you were in trouble and called out my name, I would be there to help you straight away, and come to your assistance immediately."

"Thank you for your kind consideration, Jabamiah. I'll say goodbye for now and will contact you again shortly; goodbye."

"Goodbye Lee and thank you."

HAIAHEL -   looks after those born on 11th March to 15th March.

"Haiahel, may I speak to you?"

"Lee, it is Haiahel, how are you today?"

"Quite well thanks, Haiahel. I'd like to ask you a few questions if you have time and don't mind. Firstly, are you the angel Haiahel from the House of Angels?"

"Lee, I am and I am glad to be here with you today as I have been working all night and need this break. Father has told us to give you first priority, as you need the information. Please tell the readers how I pronounce my name, as it is Hi-ah-el, with silent aitches."

"Thanks for that Haiahel, and for arriving so promptly, may I ask what you do and some of the things that you did during the night?"

"Lee it was pandemonium last night as some teenagers in a stolen car were being chased by the police. The carload of teenagers in the car hit a power pole and some were killed and this took me all night to sort out as they were very upset thinking that they were going to be punished by Father. I had to counsel them and process them and take them to their respective levels, though they are fine now."

"Haiahel, I guess they were going through a lot of confusion in their quick transition from life into death and this is a shock in itself isn't it?"

Chapter 9. House of Angels

"What's the first thing that usually goes through an accident victim's mind, especially if it happens unexpectedly?"

"Lee, the first thing that goes through their mind is usually, 'What happened? I was in an accident and thought I was hurt but there is no pain!' and, 'I'm okay!' Then they look around and see their own body and cannot associate themselves with it as it looks remote to them and not part of them and they think, 'That's me, but how? I'm here, not there!'

"Afterwards, they check their records with an angel, and then a spirit guide from the level they are assigned to, comes to take them to the light, to which they either go or refuse to."

"Haiahel, how does the spirit guide know which level to take them to?"

"The principal spirit guide assigned to them when they were alive is aware of where they are going as this guide resides on that level and is instantly informed by an angel from the House of Cherubim where all the records are kept, if this level is still current, and their records which are updated daily, are opened up to check.

"The angels are aware of the life that person has led and this is one of their roles, to look after that person when they cross over, and an angel looks at that person's scroll of life with them shortly after the time of death. Then their principal spirit guide from their spiritual level escorts them into the level of light that they have achieved during their lifetime.

"Their guardian angel goes with them too as he opens the gate and he closes the gate of that level, so that none are left to wander about. And the dead souls are made aware of their new surroundings and meet other people in spirit that they have known on earth. And they meet friends, relatives and sometimes their ancestors too."

"Haiahel, if the deceased person refuses to go to the light can their soul return to their body and regain consciousness?"

Chapter 9. House of Angels

"Lee, it can happen, but not without permission and this option is open to them if granted. And it will be in many cases and all efforts are made to do this in the case of accidental death unless it is obvious that the body cannot support life, and this is the reason they are taken away.

"But this is not what most souls really want to do, as they feel it is far better for them to remain in the spirit world that they have known before as they feel at home here, and they know where they are going to be.

"Many prefer to be here as for them it is far nicer in the light than on earth as it is less harsh and they have more say, and they have more freedom and equality; and for some it is a paradise compared to their life on earth. And also, there is usually an overwhelming, irresistible and compelling attraction urging them to come home to the light."

"Haiahel, these spirits in heaven will still be judged on Judgment Day and this is not the final resting-place for them. Can you give us an insight into what will happen to them, from here on in?"

"Lee, it is going to be a chance to enter the God plane in the Kingdom of God and the ones who are worthy will enter God's own house at the time of judgment from here. Some will reincarnate before the Day of Judgment as it is not coming just yet and they will live again; and this is an option for all of those living in the light."

"Haiahel, they soon realize the physical journey was a test and a learning process and that the reason for living was to let them attain a higher level in the light if possible. Most of them will look back with foresight and wonder at the type of lives they have led."

"Lee believe me, most cannot believe that they have led such selfish lives, as they see all, and it is then they realize that they have had wicked lives and regret it, though it was meant for their spiritual development. That is why so many lives are lived, and it is for them to develop gradually to attain a higher level of spirituality."

Chapter 9. House of Angels

"Haiahel, so it really is a gamble coming back, because, if they are too wicked to return to the light on their death, they are left on the earth plane with demons as punishment, until the Day of Judgment."

"Lee true, but it is not as big a gamble as you think because their spirit guides are there to give them daily insights and to guide them gently through life, unless they have been influenced by the wrong types, giving them wicked ideas and this influence can create havoc in their lives, destroying their chances."

"Wrong types, Haiahel? Disruptive spirits or the people they mix with?"

"Lee, it is not their own spirit guides, but evil spirits on the earth plane influencing them. And this influence is prevalent if they are susceptible to it by letting these spirits access their minds when they are under the influence of alcohol or marijuana, or other mind altering drugs.

"I would like to add that during my visits to the earth plane I have witnessed the unpleasant sight of watching people attempt self-mutilation and suicide too. I weep in sympathy for their anguish as they are going through a lot of emotional turmoil and need help. The help is sparse as many of your public hospitals, public facilities and other organizations have been closed down, so what are they to do?"

"Haiahel, we are aware of these shortcomings and we depend on our politicians for these necessities, but sadly, due to the apathy shown in society and the decline in ethical and moral standards over the last decade, the public now seem to prefer to have a good time rather than have public hospitals and adequate health care for all."

"Lee, they are victims of circumstances beyond their control and also of their own foolish actions; goodbye my friend."

"Goodbye Haiahel, and thank you for your contribution."

Chapter 9. House of Angels

MUMIAH - looks after those born on 6th March to 20th March.

"Hello Mumiah, may I have a few minutes of your time please?"

"Lee? I am Mumiah from the House of Angels and I have been expecting you to ask me some questions, and here is what I have prepared for you.

"I go about my duties with fervor and I delight in this work. My duties include going to the ends of the earth to watch out for accidents and to help out with them. I have many, many duties and they are all to help people in need, and I do this day in and day out without complaint as it is what I like doing most. And it brings me a sense of satisfaction to do it, and this is why I do it.

"This is what I enjoy and the world will not be as sad and not be as gloomy with me here as I cheer up the sick and I bring a smile to the faces of those in pain, even if they are feeling low. And it is heartening to see them smile when they are in the desperate straits they get themselves into, and to see they are still able to smile brings gladness to my heart.

"It is not the only thing I do to bring joy to others. I also tend to the gardens in our house as they are in full bloom in the springtime, and the gardens here are beautiful. And when you see them in your future travels to the spiritual realms you will soon realize who the head gardener is, and you will know who that head gardener is, because I am that head gardener!

"I also give lessons in counseling to the other angels, as I believe my skills are above theirs in this and I counsel the lost souls, and I counsel the spirits who have problems. It is wonderful to give them hope and to bring happiness into their lives and it is a wonderful feeling to see them

Chapter 9. House of Angels

regain the happiness they had lost. And I do want this as it also brings me great happiness, and it is the reason I do it.

"The reason I have told you this is that it is a joy for me too, and I want to tell the people about my duties as it involves them. I give more than I get back, as it is the way here and this is the way for some people too; and those who give, get more recognition here too and reach a higher level of spiritual awareness, as you have already told them.

"Let it be that this happens to your readers too, as they are to have firsthand knowledge, and it has been told to them for this reason; and to ignore this advice would be like throwing their hard earned wages into the garbage bin. And I want them to know and believe they are to receive wages according to their deeds, and this is so.

"Let it be seen that our Father has plans for you people that will exceed all of your expectations, and know that He loves you dearly. And do not think that you are too bad to be forgiven as Father forgives all that ask, and He has told me to remind you of this.

"Let it be known then that if you are a sinner and you have been forgiven, your life is assured but if you have not asked for forgiveness, be told that you will be cast out of Father's house, in heaven.

"Let me make it known to all of you reading this, that it is important and you will find comfort in this, knowing that by asking right now to be forgiven, that you will be."

"Well, Mumiah, that was a whirlwind of information and good advice; now can you tell me what you do in your spare time, if and when you have any?"

"Lee, it is important for me to have time to myself and this is taken regularly to unwind and reflect. I go to the church services on earth and sit in the company of the congregations and listen to the sermons with them, and I am filled with joy when all are singing hymns."

Chapter 9. House of Angels

"Let all the people understand that angels are everywhere, not just sitting in heaven in paradise; but busy doing good works all day and night, visiting the houses to see the sick and visiting hospital wards everywhere; everyday, giving comfort to the ill and dying.

"Let all know this and let all understand that we want to do this as it is our calling, not that we have to; and some have not done this but stay in the house they live in, tending it, not venturing out to do this work.

"Others look after the gates and still others are escorts for the dead souls. This takes thousands of us and there are millions of us.

"The number of guardian angels has increased due to you having had our helpers increased to as many as is needed lately, and it is evident why this is so and this is because the world is becoming too overcrowded, and this is not the best.

"We want to see all have a quality life and this is not happening, so it is our plea to ask that the people be courteous to each other, have forgiving hearts and lend a helping hand to support the starving children in the Third World, by sending gifts of food and clothing or donating money. And please go there if you have the resources to provide relief first hand as it is needed everywhere, and your presence will save lives."

"Thank you for bringing this to our attention Mumiah, and if I ever get the chance to help others overseas I will do so; goodbye for now, or do you want to say more?"

"Lee, goodbye and thank you for letting me ramble on ad-infinitum as you have been flat out keeping up to my typing. It is really efficient to use the computer keyboard like this as it eliminates the mistakes that a channeler sometimes makes when passing on information, as how can I mistake the words I type through you, myself?"

"True Mumiah, and I thank you and all of the other angels once more for the time and effort you have all put in, goodbye my friend."

Chapter 9. House of Angels

Now that we have spoken to all of the original seventy-two guardian angels from the nine houses, we will finish by looking at some of the issues that have been made quite clear to us.

I have established (at least beyond any doubt for myself) it is possible to contact and speak to God and the angels, as well as to speak to people who have died and are now in spirit.

There *is* a God who created us and has a plan for us after this life. That we survive death is one of the most significant issues for us and where we will eventually end up after death depends entirely upon our own conduct here on earth.

God *is* a living Spirit, so why is it so hard for us to believe that we will survive in spirit after death? God is immortal, so why is it so hard to believe that we as humans, in death, will not have everlasting life?

There *is* going to be a Second Coming, when the Messiah will appear, born again[21] of woman as a living human being and living on earth until his presence is made known to us, by a major event prepared by God.

There *is* going to be a judgment at the end times and those in spirit at this time will be judged in an empyreal body as spirit beings, not resurrected from the grave in a physical body as Jesus was. [22]

There *is* going to be a Rapture where the souls of the dead will rise up to meet the Lord, but this *rapture* is only for the embodiment and

---
[21] See (John 3:3)
[22] The Apostle Paul said, "It is sown a physical body, it is raised a spiritual body. If there is a physical body, there is also a spiritual body." (1 Corinthians 15:44)

Chapter 9. House of Angels

judgment of those wicked souls left in hell; that is, left on the earth plane without any physical senses, summoned for the final judgment.

There *is* a place known as hell and on Judgment Day those souls residing in hell who have led unsavory lives on earth will either remain there, be sent to the abyss, or if forgiven, be allowed to enter the light.

There are five main possibilities for souls in spirit after judgment, i.e., enter the God plane; remain in the light, reincarnate; remain in hell on the earth plane, or perish in the abyss.

Those left in the light who elect to reincarnate after judgment will be allowed to do so, but the earth's population will be greatly diminished.

Human beings living on earth during this time of judgment will remain alive and be judged after their natural life span is over.[23]

Now that we are aware of the options open to us, we should start preparing by changing our ways, leading better, more compassionate and caring lives. Not much to do really to attain everlasting life, and if we lead good lives we will end up with rewards beyond measure.

God says, "My Son will be present here to do my work with His messenger helpers. And He will be telling people about the new plans to follow. I will outline my thoughts and you will see that you are to possess special powers in spirit. And you are to become more than you ever thought possible.

---

[23] See (1 Thessalonians 4:15)

The Archangel Michael

"Hello Michael, thank you for attending."

"Lee, it is a pleasure to be here and I want to say a few words about myself first, then about our Father Yahweh, and also a few words about the future too.

"I live in the House of Archangels and we oversee the other houses as we are the messengers between God, the angels and also some messengers living on earth.

"My duties are to supervise the work carried out in the kingdom of heaven and to prepare it for the coming judgment, which will be happening within the lifetime of most of you reading this.

"My duties have been diverse and varied over the last few thousand years and it has been an onslaught of hard, backbreaking work to achieve my goals, and I have done my best.

"My work has been to take and transform the living into worthy beings for the time of judgment, and this will be sooner rather than later.

"My archenemy Satan has been shackled in chains for centuries and he is not to be allowed out now as this has been decreed by our Father, and it is His will and it is His way.

"All wickedness stems from listening to disgruntled spirits still on the earth plane and they will perish after the time of judgment. I have found that they have created most of the damage to humanity though people have said it is the work of Satan; but this is not so as he is in chains. It is the work of men that has caused this trouble on earth!

"My advice to all of you is that you are to be given one more chance to redeem yourselves before the judgment, and it is pending, so this is a warning for you to change your ways. Take heed because if you do not

The Archangel Michael

and you have sinned and not asked to be forgiven, then you will find out what hell means; and it is not going to be a birthday party, and I mean it!

"Our plans will not be thwarted and will have reached fruition with the Second Coming of the Son and He will soon take over the responsibility that has been on our shoulders for the last several thousand or so years.

"Let all who read this understand that we want the best for you, and to do this we must eliminate the worst. To accomplish this we have to have this judgment so that those left will be living in peace and harmony without fear of war or starvation, or fear of their neighbor, as is the case right now.

"Let me tell you that those living now and those dying now will see this event and it will be memorable as it is to be the biggest event that will ever take place. I will be here to supervise and my archangel peers will be here too. My earthly brothers and sisters will be helping too and many are to be told who is to do this work and they will be notified at the time.

"Let me remind you to be forgiving toward the people who persecute you and to forgive those who have trespassed into your territory and onto your property as it means little in the big picture, but means everything to you.

"My plans are to have you in one of our houses too; and we want you to be here with us, as we love you and we want to see you enjoy everlasting life with us. Our Father's biggest wish is to have this and it is my biggest wish too.

"Let me hope then that you are to be here with us to enjoy the fruits that are laid out in front of you, and your life will be rewarded beyond measure.

"Let it be known that this has been planned in advance and your life has been watched over to help you achieve this. And those who have passed over will be here to enjoy these rewards as well."

The Archangel Michael

"The judgment is to take those souls not in the light to task for their crimes, such as murder, and then after they have suffered their punishment, they will perish, unless forgiven.

"The ones in the light also have to be judged and they may be taken into the house of our Father which is the Kingdom of God. People will be judged when they die, and they will either remain on the earth plane; go into the light, go into our Father's house; reincarnate, or go into the abyss and perish.

"Those perishing can only be extinguished by Meheliah, the Angel of Death and Darkness who is given this authority by our Father. The abyss is near the earth plane and the souls of sinners are left on the earth plane until Judgment Day, and this is the waiting room; and this is where it all starts and where it all finishes for them. They are being held here as they are unworthy to enter the light and lost souls are only here because they want to be.

"Lost souls have unresolved business, but unlike most of the others, may be allowed to enter the light. It is up to individual souls if they want to reincarnate and this can be achieved at any level in the light. The others not entering the Kingdom of God can elect to remain in spirit without reincarnating and will stay at the level they have attained and given the rewards that go with that level, unless they become spirit guides."

"Michael, why do the rest of us have to have a judgment?"

"Lee, the first real people ate forbidden fruit from the Tree of Knowledge of Good and Bad, breaking one of our Father's rules by listening to the fallen angel Lucifer, described as a 'snake' by our Father. It was going to be a gift of the Tree to give them this knowledge and they partook of it beforehand."

"And now the people can do what they like, thus creating the need for a judgment, which would not have been necessary if they had not gained wisdom then.

"And the fruits of the Tree of Knowledge were only to be taken when the people were developed properly and not beforehand as Father had not finished producing humans, as He felt they were inadequate. And this is why nobody is perfect as Father wanted all to be perfect in His eyes. And He became very angry that Adam and Eve had eaten.

"And consequently, He made human life spans last only a short time from that day forward, until Judgment Day is upon us and then all those who have survived judgment will have the promised everlasting life that was supposed to be at the beginning."

"Michael, you said Father called Lucifer a snake. Didn't the symbol of a snake curled into a circle once represent everlasting life?"

"Yes Lee, the snake in a circle was a symbol used by the ancients to represent eternal life. The snake is a whole but is in itself as destructible to itself as it can be to others. To the ancients, by depicting the snake as a whole circle of completeness, it represented 'all of that is,' and it had the potential to swallow itself, thus becoming 'nothing at all,' as it was seen as all devouring. Therefore, the snake symbolized eternal life, 'all of that is' – and by eating 'all of that is', could become nothing at all.

"Adam and Eve partook of forbidden fruit from the Tree of Knowledge offered by the 'snake' Lucifer – and by eating all of that fruit forsook eternal life, returning to the dust, becoming nothing at all."

"Thank you for explaining that Michael; and to this very day most people still have a fear of snakes, an in-built primordial instinct."

"Lee, the name of our Father is Yahweh and this is His real name, not Jehovah as some call it. And it is the proper name of the God of all of that is and of all living things. Our Father is a spirit entity who was here from the gases and He was formed as you and I were formed of the gases 20 billion years ago. God came into being as a small life form and He became more with time as you are to become more with time. And He becomes more all the time as he is growing... and His knowledge is increasing as your knowledge is increasing, with time.

"This is how God is able to moderate the planet by knowing more, and He watches you and He is interested in what His loved ones such as you and the people He created are doing. God is very pleased with it all and He is always showing us His creations.

"And God is always saying how pleased He is with it, and He is always saying that the people are beautiful... and this is why He lets you all do what you will, as it pleases Him.

"God watches with interest you doing your work as He is very interested in what you all do. God is very interested in all the ways people make their habitat more comfortable. And it is His greatest pleasure to see people becoming more industrious as they are progressing to a point that they are living to a good age without discomfort. And this also pleases Him.

"I will let our Father address you now as He is prodding me with His staff and pushing in as He wants to say many things to all of you.

"Thank you for inviting me to come here today... and now, our Father in person who created heaven and earth is going to take the keyboard and type a personal message to everybody through you, His beloved messenger. Here is our Father and His name is Yahweh!"

"Thank you Michael, goodbye."

"Goodbye for now, Lee."

The Last Pages

1. I am the God who created all of you. I have been absent but am now back to watch over the world during the last days as it is nearly time, and it is going to be within your lifetime.
2. My plans include you and they are to be carried out.
3. My plans require you to have faith in me and my beloved Son who will be here to oversee the Judgment.
4. My Son is going to be here and His presence will be seen soon as He has been in preparation for your coming home and He will supervise the coming events.
5. Let me tell you that all of my faithful, living during this time will stay alive after the Judgment until they are ready to come home.
6. And the Judgment is not going to take you home before your time, but rather, to give you life forever.
7. And it will not be taken from you but given to you, as this is my plan for you who listen and embrace me and my Son.
8. My passion is to have as many of you with me as possible because you are my children and I love you, just as you love your children; so know this and believe this too.
9. Let it happen that my plans are successful and that you are part of them.
10. Let it happen that you are true to me and that you are free to come home to me without encumbrance.
11. Let me tell you that I am the one and only God and it is my wish to have you in my house with me; and I have prepared the way for you.

12. Let it be seen that you have this knowledge and that you as a responsible person want this.
    And you are to be loved and cherished.
    And this is for you and I have made great preparations for you.
    And this is why you are alive now.
    And this is why you are able to live now.
    And this is why you feel the sun and the rain.
    And this is why I have given you many gifts.
    And this is why I have made it beautiful to live.
    And this is why I want it to be as perfect for you as it can be without the wicked and the greedy, and the rest who make it difficult for you to live in peace and harmony.
13. Let it be seen that I will bring you untold gifts and give you more than you ever thought possible.
14. And all things impossible will become possible.
15. And those of you who have lost loved ones will rejoice, as you will see them again.
16. And all who have not known me in person will know me and speak to me too.
17. Let it be seen that the prophecies in the Bible will be realities too, and many have been proven beyond doubt if you check for yourself and wipe away the interpretations that scholars have provided you with for their entertainment.
18. Let me tell you that I have been waiting for you to come home to me and that I will be happier than ever to have my faithful with me in my house under my Christmas tree; and this is the tree that will bear

The Last Pages

more fruit than any other in history.

19. My love for you is unending; therefore, if you can imagine how much love you can give to those you love, you will understand how much I will give you; and you will see that I am a kind, generous and loving father to you; so do not be frightened of me as I am your friend as well as your father, and these are the best days now before the end times.
20. Let it be known that before the end, a great war will rage and this war will last for a short time then be over.
21. And the perpetrators are to be tried by my Son who will pass Judgment.
22. And he will not be lenient as the leaders have broken many rules, and my Son will not be taken in by them.
23. Let it happen then that you are told that these events will take place, and you will be told to watch out for the telltale signs which include governments giving people great lies to swallow.
24. And the wicked will be in charge in these times so be wary and be alert to it.
25. Let it be seen that my messenger will be busy during this time; so please be understanding and do not inundate him with calls for help, as he cannot; only conveying the news, not making the news.
26. He has been writing a book for these coming events called *'The Word'* and these are my words and this is what I have told him to do.
27. Let me say that I will address these issues in my book and you will have as much knowledge about me as I have about you.

The Last Pages

28. This book of mine will be published in or before the year 2008 and you will have plenty of time to read it in.
29. Let me tell you as a final blessing and a final bit of advice that my words are coming true, and anyone who thinks that I am joking know that I do not joke; and if you want to see for yourself how serious I can be, go into the wilderness and study the lions that run wild and see what they eat.
30. Let it be seen that they eat the carcasses of dead animals they have killed, and see if this is kind and see if this is compassionate and see if there is a better way; and if you find it, tell me too.
31. Let it happen that this is to be, and let it happen that you are taking this with serious consideration.
32. Let it be seen that I am also a kind and loving father to you, and let it be known that you are mine as I created you.
33. Let me tell you now that you will see me in my house, and you will be here to speak to me soon.
34. Let it be known that I love my children and that you are one of them.
35. Let me tell you that my plans are for you too and you who are reading this will be in my house with me; and I love you and I want you here with me to be one of my angels.
36. Let me tell you this is my wish, and this is going to eventuate sooner rather than later as I am here to supervise it, and I am going to start this process shortly.
37. Let it be known that my Son is going to be here soon and He will tell all of you my plans.
38. Let it be known that He is going to be known to all of you soon.

The Last Pages

39. Let me tell you that He will be here to help you and to instruct you on food distributions and He will do this for you and for me.
40. Let me tell you that I have many plans, and that you are part of them.
41. Let it be seen that you are my child and that you attend church to worship me and my Son, as we are going to be looking for you.
42. Let me tell you that this is important, as you will find out later on.
43. Let me see you in my house worshipping me soon.
44. Let it be known that you are to be given many presents and that nothing will be denied you, once you are here with me.
45. Let me tell you that I have made many things to give you, and that you are to be rewarded for your efforts in helping others.
46. Let it be seen that I am a kind and loving father who will provide for my children with all the things they desire.
47. Let me tell you that nothing will be denied you who are true to me and who loves and respects me, your father who lives in heaven and on earth.
48. Let me be your father and mother too as you need both; and as I created you from the gases I gave you life as a mother gives life, and I created all mothers too.
49. Let me tell you this; I am in the image of a man and this is my countenance for you to remember, and you will see me in my house as a kind and loving old man, and I will be here for you.
50. Let me also say this, I want you to be here with me and the effort to make it into my house is worth everything you own; and nothing is going to stop you from coming in if you are forgiven of your sins, so ask me now to forgive you, and I will.

The Last Pages

51. My Son has the key to the house and you are invited in as my guest.

52. Let me also remember to give you everlasting life as this is your main reason for living now, and that is to prove to me you are worthy of this gift that I have ready to give you.

53. Let it be known now that I have told my messengers to prepare the way for you, and to give you every direction necessary to find this; and to follow this, and to make it to your home here in the house that I have prepared for you.

54. My greatest wish is to have you with me, in this, our house; as you are more than welcome, being my child as you have been told; and what parent denies their child anything within reason?

55. Let me tell you this is a promise, and I have told you who is reading this that I am going to supply you with all your needs and give you all you desire, to live with and to play with.

56. I love you, and nothing is going to stop me from spoiling you as I crave for you to want my love and affection; and if you give me this I will give you more than you ever thought possible.

57. Let it be known that my greatest fear is that you will turn away from me without getting your rewards, and this will hurt me so do not forsake me, and I will not forsake you.

58. Let me tell you, my other children who love me will be with us too; and we will have plenty to occupy ourselves with as we have work to do, and you will be thrilled with your new work as it is to be in my name and it will be the most wonderful work that you will ever have.

59. Let me tell you that my own work is my pride and joy, and your work will be your pride and joy too; so be told this and do not think

that your life will be playing the harp all day, as it will be much better than you could ever imagine.

60. My Son is going to give you some instructions when He arrives, so let all know He is coming before the end of this generation, and we will be prepared for this wonderful event.

61. My messenger is going to help with many things for this event, and he will tell you when it is going to happen as he has been authorized to relay messages for me, and he will let you know the exact time and place my Son is going to appear.

62. My Son is my most precious gift to you. I love him and I love you. Therefore imagine how much more you will see and experience when He is here to guide you once more, to give you my blessings and to heal those with sicknesses, and to help those in need.

63. My Son is to be here to help and He will be coming with many angels, and some of those angels have written words in this book. Meet them with open arms and they will stretch theirs out to embrace you too.

64. Let it be known that this is the finish of the book now as my messenger has had to type it all, and he is going to do more work for me later on.

I will bid you farewell for now,

until we meet again,

Father.

NOTES

Glossary

Abyss — God's place reserved for those who are to perish after Judgment Day.

Angelic Records — Scrolls recording a person's present and past lives, kept in the House of Cherubim and updated on a regular basis.

Angel — Being of light, one of God's heavenly helper's.

Anointed — Officially appointed by sacred ritual.

Archangel — Messenger between God and the angels. Each one of the 'Nine Celestial Houses of Angels' has an archangel in charge of it.

Astral Plane — Non-physical boundaries of the physical universe.

Aura — Form of light energy radiating from a person's body at a frequency and color reflecting their level of spiritual awareness and their overall state of wellbeing.

Auto-type — Ability to type words received directly through the hands from a spirit entity.

Auto-write — Ability to handwrite words received directly through the hands from a spirit entity.

Glossary

Baptism — Religious sacrament: Usually performed by pouring water over the head or even by a full immersion of the body, to become a member of a church, or to be recognized as a Christian.

Book of Life — God's personal diary.

Canticle — Chanting of biblical text or hymn used in a church service.

Celestial — Heavenly - divine.

Channeler — Person who can communicate with spirit entities.

Christening — Name giving ceremony and acceptance into the Christian church; usually includes baptism.

Cupid — Mythological Cherub whose role is to bring people together romantically.

Demon — Often used in reference to an evil spirit which is the soul of a deceased person remaining on the earth plane, but actually, a demon is a fallen angel.

Destiny — Reincarnates are able to choose their future destiny before birth; however this can be changed by accident, crime or by any other circumstance which may alter the course of their pre-determined life.

Glossary

Earth Plane Spiritual realm: The waiting room for the majority of deceased souls who are to enter the abyss on Judgment Day. Commonly known as purgatory.

Empyreal Body Body formed from pure light energy, pertaining to the regions of heaven.

Evil Spirit Soul of a wicked person unworthy of going to the light, left on the earth plane until Judgment Day

God Supreme Being: Creator of heaven and earth; Creator of all things great and small, also known as Yahweh. YHWH in Hebrew.

God Plane God's personal house: The residence of the Trinity, reserved for the pure of heart, after Judgment Day.

Golaiah An earthly female messenger between the angels, spirits and people, to assist at the time of judgment.

Guardian Angel An angel with orders to watch over specific people and specific parts of the earth.
Every person has a guardian angel assigned to them at the time of birth.

Heaven Five spiritual realms in the light, where spirits reside and await judgment.

Glossary

Hell — See earth plane: A spiritual realm not in the light where wicked deceased souls await for Judgment.

Helper — Angel helper to one of the guardian angels or archangels.

Higher-Self — The collective-unconscious of a person's soul which has a conscious memory of all past-lives lived that will be viewed and restored at the time of judgment.

Holy Spirit — Breath of life and healing imparted by God to humans and all living things.

Judgment Day — The time people will be judged to determine which spiritual realm they are to be assigned to. Judgment Day will last for one thousand years.

Kingdom of God — All of the physical and spiritual realms including the nine houses of angels and the God plane.

Kingdom of Heaven — The Light: The five spiritual realms in the light, not including the nine houses of angels, the earth plane or the God plane.

Lost Soul — Soul that remains on the earth plane because of unresolved earthly matters. A lost soul may be allowed to enter the light at anytime, if deemed worthy.

Glossary

Medium Person, who in a light trance allows the words of a deceased person to speak out through their mouth, enabling that spirit to communicate with the living.

Messenger Person or angel who delivers messages to the people from the spiritual realms.

My House Yahweh's reference to the God plane.

NDE Near death experience, a person deemed clinically dead who has returned to life.

Oanedus An earthly messenger between God, archangels; the angels, the spirits and people.

Rapture Embodiment of wicked souls on the earth plane to be raised from hell for judgment.

Reincarnation Transition of the soul from an empyreal body in the light to a new physical body on earth.

Resurrection Provision of a temporary empyreal body at the time of judgment for souls remaining on the earth plane. These souls (including lost souls) are to be provided with an empyreal body to be judged in.
Spirits residing in the light already have this empyreal body. Resurrection will not be the resuscitation of a dead body nor is it to be provision of a new physical body. (See reincarnation)

Glossary

Satan — Fallen angel from the House of Cherubim banished from the kingdom of heaven, now residing on the earth plane awaiting judgment.

Second Coming — The Parousia: The return of God's Son, born once again on earth in a physical body for the second coming, to restore peace and harmony on earth before the beginning of Judgment Day.

Son — Jesus of Nazareth: Known as the Son of God, Son of David; Son of man, the Messiah or Christ.

Soul — Consciousness of a living person or that of a deceased person left on the earth plane, not residing in the light.

Spirit — Deceased soul residing in the light.

Spirit Guide — Spirit who guides a living person on earth and helps with their transition into the spirit world at death.

The Light — Five spiritual realms: The light is not inclusive of the abyss, the earth plane, the nine houses of angels or the God plane. (See pages 2-5)

Index

A

Abraham, xxv
Abyss, xx, 116, 189, 192
Adam, 193
Addict, 36, 100
Administrator, 13, 18, 68, 144
Afghanistan, 69, 143, 168
Angelic Records, 27, 35, 92, 94, 160, 173
Angel of Change, 133
Angel of Death, 96, 116, 119, 192
Angel of Good, 133
Angel of Healing, 168
Angel of Health and Vitality, 149
Angel of Human Affairs, 168
Angel of Industry, 133
Angel of Light, 133
Angel Luhian, x
Angel of Mercy, 98
Angel of Prosperity, 133
Angel of Supply, 167
Angel of the Lord, 13, 16, 24, 26, 109, 164
Angel of Time, 140
Anointed, 99
Apostle Paul, 188
Apocalyptic, 145
Archangel Gabriel, 6, 21, 166

Archangel Meheliah, 96, 116, 119, 192
Archangel Michael, 6, (190-194)
Archangel Omni, xxiii,
Archbishop, 121
Astral plane, 4, 5
Atmosphere, 74, 126, 161, 176, 178
Aura, 157, 158
Australia, viii, xvi, xxii, xxiv, 153
Authority, 33, 92, 119, 121, 155, 192
Authorized, 25, 33, 95, 99, 201
Automatic-typing, 3, 41, 118
Automatic-writing, 3, 41

B

Baptism, 123
Beginning, xxv, xxvii, 1, 10, 21, 80, 84, 97, 146, 149, 193
Bible, 3, 36, 42, 52, 196
Birth, 5, 23, 48, 50, 121, 122
Birth control, 121, 122
Blessed, 14, 58, 66, 120, 133, 134, 139,
Blessing /s, 72, 164, 198, 201
Book of Life, 129

Index

C

Catholic, 114
Celestial, xvii -xix, 6, 7 -9, 27
Ceremony, 78, 122, 123
Ceremony of Cleansed Souls, 78
Channel, 1-4, 9, 27, 169, 187
Charioteers, 22, 120
Chief Counselor of Lost Souls, 76
Child, 10, 22, 81, 123, 165, 199 200
Children, xxvii, xxviii, 22, 23, 42, 50, 58, 61, 64, 88, 106, 121-123, 134, 147, 153, 187, 195, 198, 199, 200
Choir, 15, 115
Christ, 52, 53, 117, 129
Christen, 122, 123
Christian, 80, 99, 114, 122, 123, 129, 157
Christmas tree, 196
Church, 52, 53, 69, 121, 122, 125 -128, 186, 199
Church leaders, 52, 124, 125
Clairvoyance, 3, 4
Cleanse, 77, 78, 120
Collective-unconscious, 172
Communicate, 2, 3, 6, 9, 62, 85, 117, 159, 172

Communion, 126
Concerts, 49, 80
Counsel, 1, 28, 75, 102, 124, 174, 181, 185
Create, 22, 53, 57, 73, 96, 103, 111, 117, 118, 133, 143, 148, 159, 170, 176, 177, 184
Created, ix, xxviii, 29, 63, 74, 95, 104, 106, 110, 119, 123, 157, 173, 188, 190, 194, 195, 198, 199
Creator, 97, 117
Cupid, 65

D

Dead, 20, 32, 38, 46, 78, 99, 115, 116, 182, 187, 188, 198
Death, x, 1, 12, 21, 23, 46, 47, 63, 64, 78, 88, 94, 98, 103, 105, 116, 119, 145, 151, 172, 181-184, 188
Death penalty, 81, 153
Democratic society, 57
Demon/s, 1, 3, 81, 88, 96, 116, 119, 159, 171, 172, 174, 184
Demonic possession, 95
Denominations, 129
Destiny, 60, 61, 104
Deuteronomy, 3

Index

Die, 4, 12, 39, 41, 50, 59, 60, 63, 87, 94, 98, 100, 107, 114, 116, 129, 139, 148, 153, 165, 167, 188, 192

Disaster, 8, 52, 62, 103, 104, 137, 142, 144, 167, 179

Distribution, 43, 44, 127, 199

Divorce, 35, 36

Dying, 41, 46, 49, 50, 81, 98, 150, 174, 187, 191

E

Earth, viii, 1, 5, 7, 10, 17, 20, 22, 27, 34, 35, 47, 49, 50, 71, 74, 75, 82, 86, 87, 89, 90, 97, 99, 102 - 104, 107, 108, 115, 117, 119 - 121, 123, 130, 131, 133, 135, 140, 144, 145, 152, 156, 159, 162, 163, 173, 174, 176, 177, 182, 183, 185, 186, 188 -190, 194, 199

Earth bound, 1, 3, 161, 162

Earthly messenger, 16, 98, 99

Earth plane, 1, 2, 4, 13, 29, 32 - 34, 38, 48, 63, 75, 77, 88, 89, 96, 98, 100, 102, 114, 115, 116, 117, 119, 145, 158, 159, 172 -174, 184, 188, 189, 190, 192

Earthquake, 52, 142

Ecclesiastes, 46

Economy, 30, 31, 43, 65, 111, 131, 143, 147

Egypt, 64, 92, 119

Empyreal body, 145, 188

End, xxvii, 25, 26, 29, 32, 35, 36, 38, 46, 70, 80, 97, 104, 110, 114, 115, 145, 146, 148, 168, 169, 188, 189, 197, 201

English, 67, 132, 170

Enlightenment, xx, xxiii, 2, 4, 14, 16, 37, 76

Entity, 3, 9, 29, 96

Environment, 9, 20, 74, 84, 155, 176, 178

Environment Protection Authority, (EPA), 155

Eternal life, 193

Euthanasia, 50

Eve, 193

Everlasting, xxvii, 65, 188, 189, 191, 193, 200

Evil, 34, 38, 58, 70, 83, 143, 144

Evil spirits, 1, 29, 96, 116, 117, 119, 159, 172, 184

Execution, 153

Exodus, 119

Exorcism, 96, 119

Extinguish, xxvii, 58, 96, 119, 172, 192

Index

F

Fallen angel, 1, 29, 192
Father, ix, xxi, 11, 12, 15 -18, 20, 21, 23 -27, 29, 30, 33, 34, 37- 44, 51, 53, 55, 56, 61, 63 - 67, 69 -72, 77- 82, 84, 87, 89, 95 - 97, 99 -107, 109, 112, 114, 116, 117, 119, 122, 123, 126 -130, 132, 133, 135, 138, 139,145 -148, 152, 154, 155, 157, 158, 162, 164, 165, 168 - 178, 181, 186, 190 -194, 197 -199, 201
Famine, 18, 103, 138, 148
Final, xxviii, 4, 14, 35, 36, 39, 82, 183, 189, 198
Fire, xxii, 18, 49, 63, 81, 103, 142, 145, 159
Flood, 18, 29, 103, 107, 142
Font, 13
Forbidden fruit, 192, 193
Foreign Aid, 44, 148
Forgive/n, xxiii, 20, 33, 39, 64, 77, 78, 90, 100, 101, 111, 113, 129, 173, 186, 189, 191, 192, 200
Forgiveness, xxiii, 101, 186
Fortuneteller, 37
Frequency, 157, 158

G

Gases, 44, 45, 106, 155, 177, 178, 194, 199
Gatekeeper, 20
Gate/s, 7, 11, 102, 182, 187
Geriatric Center, 59
Ghost/s, 33, 161, 162
God Plane, xx, 2, 4, 5, 7, 86, 107, 129, 183, 189
God's Words, xxi, xxv 10, 11, 22, 34, 38, 53, 54, 71, 88, 97, 117, 118, 121, 123, 140, 158, 164, 189, 195
Golaiah, 16, 27, 30, 58, 134, 135, 166
Government/s, 43, 65, 137, 138, 143, 144, 148, 154, 176, 197
Greece, 64
Greenhouse Gases, 155
Guardian Angel, x, (xi-xv), (xvii-xix), 1, 5 -11, 22, 27, 38, 43, 48, 51, 54, 67, 71-73, 77, 85, 88, 97, 102, 103, 116, 121, 125, 128, 135, 140, 164, 166, 170, 180, 182, 187, 188
Guard, 11, 22, 50, 51, 55, 73, 142

Index

H

Harp, 14, 66, 115, 201

Healing, 11, 41, 42, 99, 168

Health, 41, 147, 149 -151, 184

Heaven, 4, 6, 10, 29, 40, 45, 49, 75, 79, 97, 108, 109, 115, 117, 119, 142, 145, 152, 183, 186, 187, 194, 199

Heavenly, viii, 1, 6, 31, 40, 48, 49, 65, 68, 86, 96, 100, 109, 157, 160

Hell, 32, 38, 89, 90, 98, 106, 174, 189, 191

Helpers, 7, 8, 14, 15, 17, 23, 26, 41, 51, 67, 69, 79, 82, 116, 131, 140, 169, 170, 171, 174, 176, 187, 189

Hierarchy of Angels, 2, 7

Higher-self, 94, 95, 123, 160, 172, 173

Holy, 122, 123, 128, 139, 166

Holy Communion, 126

Holy Spirit, 41, 42

House of Angels, xv, xix, xx, 157, (164-189)

House of Archangels, xiv, xix, xx, 21, (140-163), 190

House of Cherubim, xi, xvii, xx, 20, (22-37), 78, 182

House of Dominions, xii, xviii, xx, (54-70)

House of Nephilim, 29

House of Powers, xiii, xviii, xx, (88-120)

House of Principalities, xiv, xix, xx, (121-139)

House of Seraphim, x, xi, xvii, xx, (11-21)

House of Thrones, xii, xvii, xx, (38-53)

House of Virtues, xiii, xviii, xx, (71-87)

Hospital, 13, 184, 187

Human/s, 3, 5, 29, 39, 48, 82, 94, 95, 104, 106, 111, 127, 133, 156, 161, 167, 168, 188, 193

Human being/s, 1, 5, 26, 28, 48, 125, 188, 189

Humanity, 63, 64, 111, 118, 131, 140, 164, 190

Humankind, xxv, 62, 70, 122, 151

Human race, 15, 69, 74, 99, 111, 167

Hymns, 49, 53, 78, 126, 127, 186

I

Image, xxviii, 159, 199

Incarnation, 27, 88

Index

Instructions, 18, 38, 40, 73, 135, 199, 201
Instruments, 14, 49, 66, 78, 108, 110
Intruder, 96
Intuition, 72, 73, 170
Iraq, 70, 168
Isaac, xxv
Israel, 83

J

Jacob, xxv
Jehovah, 193
Jesus, vi, xvi, xxv, 36, 52, 64, 99, 129, 165, 188
Jew, 114
John, 94, 188
Joseph, 64
Judge, 25, 81, 145
Judged, 14, 29, 33, 77, 78, 83, 94, 112, 113, 114, 129, 145, 183, 188, 189, 192
Judgment, ix, 5, 27, 38, 39, 44, 46, 51, 57, 62 - 64, 69, 78, 82, 83, 87, 89, 90, 94, 96, 97, 99, 101, 104, 107, 112 -114, 116, 117, 119, 123, 129, 135, 143, 145, 149, 161, 172, 173, 175, 183, 184, 188 -193, 195, 197

K

Kill, 48, 50, 54, 56, 60, 64, 69, 81, 90, 119, 153, 164, 181, 198
Kingdom of God, xx, 4, 5, 33, 129, 183, 192
Kingdom of Heaven, 5, 51, 52, 86, 123, 129, 161, 190
King Herod, 64
King Solomon, 46

L

Last days, 39, 82, 101, 117, 195
Last Word and Testament, 80, 87, 118
Leaders, 70, 99, 118, 121, 133, 138, 168, 197
Level One, 2, 4
Level Two, 4, 168
Level Three, 4
Level Four, 4
Level Five, 4
Level Six, 4, 129, 159
Level Seven, 2, 4, 5, 76
Level of Competence, xxvi, xx, 4
Level of Enlightenment, xx, 4, 76
Level of Higher Learning, xx, 4, 86, 159
Level of Introduction, xx, 4, 33
Level of Settlement, xx, 4
Levitation, 1

Index

Library, 92

Light, 1-5, 7, 9, 16, 20, 25, 28, 29, 32-34, 39, 43, 50, 75, 76, 78, 89, 90, 98, 99, 111, 113 -116, 119 -121, 127, 129, 133, 158, 161, 162, 172, 173, 179, 182 -184, 189, 192

Longevity, xxvii

Lord, 13, 16, 24, 26, 109, 164, 188

Lost soul, 1, 4, 33, 34, 75 -77, 161, 162, 185, 192

Lucifer, 192, 193

M

Marriage, 35, 36, 121, 122

Mars, 33

Mary, 64

Matthew, 36, 52, 144

Meditating, 160

Meditation, 4

Messages, 12, 22, 24, 67, 85, 103, 134, 147, 194, 201

Messenger, ix, x, 1, 5, 6, 12, 16, 24, 27, 30, 33, 44, 58, 67, 90, 96, 98, 99, 103, 110, 116, 119, 124, 126, 135, 140, 146, 189, 190, 194, 197, 200, 201

Messiah, 99, 188

Metaphysics, 1

Middle East, 64, 70, 143, 168

Miracle, 71, 72, 86, 99

Mortal, 62

Moses, 3, 119

Mother Earth, 115

Mother Nature, 146, 171

Muslim, 114

N

Napoleon, 63

Near death experience, 32

Nephilim, 29

Nero, 173

Nine Houses of Angels, (xi -xv) (xvii - xx), 6, 7, 21, 94, 131, 188

O

Oanedus, 157

Old Hebrew, 83, 84, 170

Ollse, 2, 4

Omnipresent, 62

Ouija board, 172

Out of body experience, 32

Ozone layer, 138, 155

P

Palliative care, 171

Paradise, 183

Paranormal, 1

Past-lives, 27, 28, 91, 93, 94, 95, 160, 163, 172

Index

Perish, 33, 63, 64, 82, 90, 104, 105, 107, 114, 117, 119, 158, 173, 189, 190, 192

Peter, 52, 145, 146

Phenomenon, 96

Physical, 5, 15, 23, 29, 35, 48, 56, 88, 108, 111, 150, 151, 160 - 162, 170, 174, 183, 188, 189

Pit, 82, 83, 90

Planet, 54, 74, 143, 156, 176, 178, 194

Polar caps, 177, 178

Politics, 48, 61, 101, 124 -126, 131, 139, 184

Pollution, 34, 74, 146, 155, 170, 177

Pope, 121

Possess, xxiii, 96, 119, 189

Possessed, 96, 172

Possession, 95, 96, 122, 138

Prayer, 11, 20, 25, 33, 34, 41, 42, 53, 63, 70 -72, 77, 78, 81, 82, 101, 112, 127, 128, 141, 165, 167 168, 173

Present-self, 94

Priest, 96

Principal spirit guide, 2, 182

Prison, 112 -114, 117, 153,

Prisoners, 112, 113

Promiscuity, 122

Prophecies, 64, 70, 196

Prophet, 3, 16

Protestant, 114

Psychic, x, 5, 9, 12, 96

Punish, 13, 25, 33, 58, 70, 96, 100, 118, 173, 181

Punishment, 13, 34, 63, 64, 116, 184, 192

R

Rapture, 145, 188

Records, 3, 11, 20 -22, 27, 32, 35, 42, 56, 78, 80, 82, 91, 92, 94, 101, 105, 113, 123, 129, 154, 157, 160, 173, 182

Recycling, 176

Redeem, 39, 190

Refuge, 64, 84, 136

Reincarnate, 7, 29, 173, 183, 189, 192,

Religion, 36, 38, 114, 121, 124, 126, 129

Resurrection, 26, 47

Revelation, 25, 94, 118, 144

Reward, xxviii 17, 25, 39, 45, 58, 65, 69, 129, 134, 176, 189, 191, 192, 199, 200

Rome, 64

Ryan, Ronald. 153

Index

S

Saint, 165
Satan, 82, 116-118, 190,
Saved, ix, x, 63, 89, 90, 92, 104, 107, 120, 153, 165
Scientists, 176
Scroll, 18, 55, 56, 67, 68, 80, 84, 101, 102, 173, 182
Second Coming, 188, 191
Second death, 39, 96, 90, 97, 116
Second World War, 42
Sects, 114
Seers, 16
Sentry, 11, 20
Sermon, 14, 126, 127, 129, 186
Seventh heaven, 4
Sexually transmitted diseases, (STD's), 122
Sin, 20, 30, 38, 58, 77, 78, 89, 101, 105, 114, 129, 200
Sinned, 20, 39, 89, 191
Sinner, 34, 90, 174, 186, 192
Sixth sense, 170
Slavery, 57
Snake, 192, 193
Son, vi, xxv, 10, 52, 53, 99, 114, 129, 145, 189, 191, 195, 197-201

Soul, 1- 5, 7, 11-13, 17, 20, 28, 32-34, 38, 63, 76 -78, 84, 95-99, 102, 107, 108, 114, 115, 116, 119, 120, 123, 127, 145, 162, 172 -174, 182, 187-189, 192
Soul mate, 163
South East Asia, 143
Spirit, 1-3, 9, 11, 14, 19 -21, 27, 28, 32, 33, 78, 86 -89, 94, 100 - 102, 107, 108, 110, 114, 119, 120, 157-159, 161-163, 171-174, 182 -185, 188 -190, 192
Spirit entity, 94, 193
Spirit guide, 1, 2, 5, 11, 13, 20, 32, 34 -37, 46, 85, 98, 108, 113, 167, 170, 173, 174, 182, 184, 192
Spiritism, 3
Spirit medium, 3, 9, 32, 33, 172
Spirit of Blindness, 41
Spirit of Deafness, 41
Spiritual, xxiii, 15, 23, 46, 60, 95, 123, 168, 183
Spiritual awareness, xxv, 2, 3, 6, 14, 20, 78, 129, 186
Spiritual enlightenment, xxiii, 37
Spirituality, 4, 183
Spiritual level, 4, 46, 182

Index

Spiritual realm, xx, xxv, 2, 4, 6, 7, 9 -11, 20, 21, 26, 27, 31, 33, 39, 48, 49, 62, 68, 77, 86, 88, 93.-96, 100 -102, 116, 119, 131, 134, 158 -60, 168, 172, 174, 185
Spiritual rebirth, 123
Spirit world, 2, 12, 32, 33, 37, 84, 114, 123, 172, 174, 183
Suicide, 96, 184
Symbol, 193

T
Telepathy, 2, 3, 5
Terminally ill, 46
Tesla, Nikola, 74
Test, xxvi, 2, 5, 86, 89, 135, 183
Thessalonians, 189
The Word, ix, 25, 26, 80,197
Third World, 187
Timekeeper, 141
Trance, 3
Tree of Knowledge, 192, 193
Tsunami, 52, 142

U
Unclean spirit, 13, 95, 119, 158
Universe, 10, 76, 86, 106, 131
Unworthy, 32, 174, 192

V
Virgin Mother, 64, 165
Volcano, 52

W
Walk-in, 94, 95, 96
War, 8, 42, 54, 63, 64, 69, 125, 142, 144, 148, 154, 168, 191,197
Wedlock, 121-123
Western World, 25
White light, 9, 43
Wicked, 51, 58, 64, 82, 89, 101, 105, 144, 153, 174, 183, 184, 189, 190, 196, 197
Wilderness, 48, 101, 198
World, xxv, 8, 10, 23 -25, 28, 30, 45, 50, 54, 58, 60, 61, 64, 82, 84, 87, 101, 104, 105, 107-109, 111, 120, 125, 128, 133, 136, 137, 144, 146, 147, 149, 151, 155, 161, 162, 167, 168, 170, 175, 177, 180, 185, 187, 195
World leaders, xxv, 24, 44, 82, 121, 124, 131, 132
World Trade Center, 39
Worship, 53, 128, 129, 199
Worthy, xxi, xxviii, 32, 42, 53, 73, 114, 121, 173-175, 183, 190, 200

Y
Yahweh, viii, ix, xxiv, xxv, xxviii, 6 - 8, 18, 53, 79, 80, 83, 86, 87, 95, 97, 99, 117-119, 123, 158, 166, 175, 190, 193, 194

Bibliography

Yahweh, God of all things great and small

The Order of Guardian Angels

The Messenger Oanedus

Archangel Gabriel

Archangel Michael

Archangel Omni

Spirit Guide Ollse

The Holy Bible

Endnote

The author hopes you have found this little book enlightening. It will make your stomach bitter, but it will be as sweet as honey in your mouth.

All care has been taken to reproduce the given names of the guardian angels herein to a known standard wherever possible, following as far as pronunciation permits, other similar lists of names published.

Disclaimer.

Even though the names of angels and dates provided in this book appear online and in numerous other publications, all have been personally reconfirmed by the author at the time of writing and approved by each angel channeled herein.

Other books by this author.

The Word: God's Last Word and Testament. 2012
Lulu Press Inc.

Both books are available in print from all major booksellers, or order your book online from Lulu.com, Amazon.com or Barnes and Noble.com.
A preview of various chapters is also readily available on Google.

www.ingramcontent.com/pod-product-compliance
Lightning Source LLC
Chambersburg PA
CBHW050138170426
43197CB00011B/1886